Books by Robert Giroux

A Deed of Death   1990

The Book Known as Q   1982
A Consideration of Shakespeare's Sonnets

The Education of an Editor   1981
R. R. Bowker Memorial Lecture

A Deed of Death

Robert Giroux

The Story Behind

the Unsolved Murder

of Hollywood Director

William Desmond Taylor

A Deed of Death

Alfred A. Knopf

New York

1990

THIS IS A BORZOI BOOK
PUBLISHED BY ALFRED A. KNOPF, INC.

Copyright © 1990 by Robert Giroux

*All rights reserved under International and Pan-American Copyright
Conventions. Published in the United States by Alfred A. Knopf, Inc.,
New York, and simultaneously in Canada by Random House of Canada
Limited, Toronto. Distributed by Random House, Inc., New York.*

Library of Congress Cataloging-in-Publication Data

Giroux, Robert.
    A deed of death : the story behind the unsolved murder of
Hollywood director William Desmond Taylor / Robert Giroux. — 1st
ed.
      p. cm.
    Bibliography: p.
    Includes index.
    ISBN 0-394-58075-3
    1. Taylor, William Desmond, 1872–1922.   2. Motion picture
producers and directors—United States—Biography.   3. Murder—
California—Los Angeles—Case studies.   I. Title.
HV6534.L7G57   1990
364.1′523′0979493—dc20   89-30451   CIP

Manufactured in the United States of America
First Edition

The movie industry offered rewards for the apprehension of Taylor's slayer—and trembled, lest the solution prove worse than the mystery.

TERRY RAMSAYE

We used to think Taylor was queer for young girls, because we didn't know he was a reformer trying to save them, a sort of father figure.

ALLAN DWAN

The movie bosses . . . were anxious to suppress the whole thing. They'd rather sacrifice Taylor than sacrifice the whole industry.

KING VIDOR

Contents

Illustrations

Illustrations

Illustrations

Illustrations

Preface

THIS IS a book about an unsolved murder. It is also in part a book about the early movies—the silents —and the people who made them. The murder of William Desmond Taylor, a leading motion picture director at Paramount, occurred early in 1922, when I was seven. Researching this book has been almost a work of archaeology.

I loved the movies from childhood. One of the first films I saw, at age five or six, was a Charlie Chaplin comedy. When my older sister and I emerged into the sunlight after the Saturday matinee, there was Charlie in person on the street—derby hat, little black mustache, baggy trousers, big shoes, flexible cane. I was overjoyed and watched him cavort about until my sister dragged me home. When I told my parents about it excitedly, my sister cut in scornfully: "Don't you realize that he wasn't the *real* Charlie Chaplin?" I was dumbfounded; the figure in the street looked exactly like Charlie. If he could materialize on a screen in the theater, why not in the street as well? It was a long time, a whole week, before I was convinced otherwise: I saw two pseudo-Chaplins, side by side, imitating the master. It was an early lesson in the problem of distinguishing reality from appearance. This distinction happens to be one of the chief difficulties with the Taylor case.

Vicarious involvement with the history of the movies continued to recur throughout my life. In 1939, the film and art historian Jay Leyda, who worked at the Film Library of the Museum of Modern Art in New York, introduced me, a newly employed book editor, to a French cameraman who had taken part in one of the earliest movies ever made. He was François Doublier, who, in the 1890s, while in his teens, had worked in the photographic laboratories of Louis and Auguste Lumière. Doublier, living in America and working for the Pathé film company, wanted to write a book about his experiences, and I wanted to publish it; unfortunately, it never got written. I had seen the early film *Workers Leaving the Lumière Factory* (1895). As the big wooden gates of the factory in Lyons opened, a group of young girls in long skirts, flat little straw hats, and blouses with leg-o'-mutton sleeves poured out onto the cobblestoned street, while a boy on a wobbly bicycle, bringing up the rear, gesticulated wildly before falling to the ground. "I am that boy!" said Doublier, who invited me to see his workshop in Fort Lee, New Jersey. There he showed me one of the first Lumière cameras, a compact work of art in itself—a portable box made of fine polished wood, with protective brass corners and a brass handle that folded into a brass niche. This triple marvel served alternately as recording camera, printing machine, and projector. (In the same years Thomas Edison's movie camera weighed almost a ton; it could be moved only on a circular track, revolving to catch sunlight at the Black Maria studio in West Orange, New Jersey, to which performers were required to journey in order to be filmed.) In the 1890s, the Lumière brothers had sent young Doublier and other craftsmen with their portable cameras all over Europe. They shot brief *actualités* of local sights and inhabitants wherever they happened to be, developed them in their hotel bathtubs, and projected the films on makeshift screens the same evening, charging pennies for admission. Doublier himself had gone to Russia in 1896 to film the coronation of Czar Nicholas—a film that Leo Tolstoy saw.* Through Doublier, I felt I had made contact with the very beginnings of this twentieth-century art form.

In the 1950s, when Hollywood was undergoing a sociological sea change because of television, I met King Vidor, one of the great directors during Hollywood's golden age. I worked with him as editor while he wrote his autobiography, which was published in 1953.† We often talked about the Taylor murder case, which became one of his obsessions, perhaps because the victim, like himself, was a director. He introduced me to Gloria Swanson, who had known William Desmond Taylor. Vidor also arranged for a telephone interview with Mary Pickford, three of whose films Taylor had directed. Confined to bed, Miss Pickford free-associated for nearly an hour in a relaxed conversation. In New York, I had met the silent-screen star Blanche Sweet; we were fellow members and

* See Jay Leyda, *Kino: A History of the Russian and Soviet Film* (New York: Macmillan, 1960), and Félix Mesguich, *Tours de Manivelle* (Paris: Grasset, 1933).

† King Vidor, *A Tree Is a Tree* (New York: Harcourt, Brace, 1953).

directors of the National Board of Review of Motion Pictures, an early civic body dating from 1909, which fought movie censorship from the start. Miss Sweet had started in the movies under D. W. Griffith and had married the silent-film director Marshall Neilan, a close friend of Taylor's. They all had important roles in film history and were generous in answering my questions about the murdered director.

The more information I collected about the Taylor case over thirty years, the more puzzling it seemed. Even well-known connoisseurs of crime, like the writers Georges Simenon and Erle Stanley Gardner, found it baffling. When I finally grasped the concealed and probably covered-up meaning of what had happened, I also understood why the murder was never solved. It seems unlikely, after almost seventy years, that the name of the murderer—a hired hit man—will ever be known, but this book shows *why* Taylor was killed.

It also shows why, in 1922, the case was not pursued more intelligently and effectively. In the wake of his murder, William Desmond Taylor (né William Cunningham Deane-Tanner) was vilified as a seducer of young actresses and at the same time pictured as a homosexual. Research into his past in Ireland, England, Canada, and America has produced a different profile of this well-born, disinherited, struggling soldier of fortune.

The case involves two flamboyant screen stars, Mabel Normand and Mary Miles Minter. Young and beautiful, without education, both women had been catapulted to national fame and fortune. After Taylor's murder, they talked and talked to reporters and interviewers, and a good part of their stories is reproduced in their own colorful language. They both "looked up to" the experienced and sophisticated Taylor as to a father, and at the same time were very much in love with him. It is clear that on his part, he loved Mabel only; it cost him his life. Meanwhile his position at Paramount forced him to "be nice to" Mary Miles Minter, who seized on this and accepted it as love. The principals in the case seemed often to be living lives of fantasy, not unlike the dramas they created on the screen; they had trouble at times determining which life was the real one.

In the 1920s, the national demand for fantasy fodder was at a high point. The enormous moviegoing public found food for their fantasies in the hundreds of films released each year. In 1921, over six hundred U.S. movies were produced. Television of course did not exist; radio had barely started as a national entertainment medium. The public also found gobs of fantasy fodder in the popular fan magazines, on newsstands everywhere, dedicated to the glorification of the stars and filled with fabricated and inflated gossip.

The American preference for myth and fantasy over dull facts clearly influenced some reporters in their treatment of the Taylor murder case. They not only acted as purveyors of movieland fantasy but manufactured it, in the hope of "making news." Perhaps the most incredible example was the farce staged at Taylor's grave by a woman reporter who was convinced that Henry Peavey, Taylor's black valet, was guilty of the murder. She thought she could obtain a confession by frightening the innocent man; details are given in the chapter on Taylor's household. Also in the realm of fantasy was Mary Miles Minter's "dialogue" with Taylor's corpse in the mortuary, which is reproduced in her own words in the chapter on her career.

Newspapers found the Taylor case a tremendous stimulus to increased circulation, in large part owing to the Hollywood setting. One movie executive, Benjamin B. Hampton, wrote that a newspaper editor told him "the Taylor stories sold more newspapers everywhere in America than were ever sold by any item of news, not excepting war news, before or since"—that is, by 1931, when his book was published.* Hampton, a literate executive in the film business, educated at Harvard, had joined the finance department of Paramount and had an intelligent interest in and curiosity about the goings-on. His book, written at the urging of Dr. John Dewey of Columbia University, is one of a handful of reliable sources for the period.

"Hollywood" had become national, and to some extent international, news during World War I, when stars like Mary Pickford, Douglas Fairbanks, Mabel Normand, and especially Charlie Chaplin took part in war bond rallies and military enlistment drives. Charlie's comedy *Shoulder Arms* was wildly popular with troops everywhere. Mabel, who was unnerved at having to meet the First Lady at the premiere of Samuel Goldwyn's *Joan of Plattsburg*, in which she was starred, told her friends with surprise that "Mrs. Woodrow Wilson was lovely to me."

As more and more details of the earlier life of William Desmond Taylor emerged in the press, they seemed to mislead and confuse reporters and readers and to make it more difficult to understand what had happened. The

* Benjamin B. Hampton, *A History of the Movies* (New York: Covici-Friede, 1931), p. 286.

young Anglo-Irishman's drifting after he ran away from home, his married life in New York, his desertion of his family, his career on the stage, his adventures in Alaska and Canada, even his change of name for theatrical reasons, seemed to scandalize readers and editorialists. Journalists expecting the details of Taylor's life to provide clues to a solution of the murder found that they led—as far as the identity of the killer was concerned—nowhere. Taylor, who lived in what has misleadingly been called the Age of Innocence, faced years of struggle to maintain his existence before he "made it" in Hollywood.

There is a key to the mystery of the Taylor murder case: the era in which it happened. The early twenties—the years following the trauma and shock of the First World War—were the times when the American public voted for Prohibition, while the national consumption of liquor became heavier than ever; an era in which many ordinary people were elevated to unaccustomed affluence and importance as "stars"; and a period in which there emerged in Hollywood circles and in a few big cities a rampant postwar drug culture, not fully known to the general public. Making sense of the Taylor murder case is possible only if all these elements are taken into account. Finally, it was the era of the coming of age of the century's new art form—the movies—during one of the craziest and most colorful periods of American history.

A Deed of Death

1

Death in Alvarado Court

As her limousine pulled away from the curb at the entrance of Alvarado Court, Mabel Normand turned around to the back window and blew kisses to Bill Taylor, who was standing on the entrance steps, waving goodbye. On an impulse—and Mabel was nothing if not impulsive —she pressed her lips to the window, leaving a trace of lipstick. Taylor returned her affectionate gesture, blowing kisses until her car was out of sight. It was ten minutes or so before 8:00 p.m. on Wednesday, February 1, 1922, as Taylor walked back to his apartment to meet his death.

Shortly after midnight, Mabel's best friend, Edna Purviance, returning from a party, saw the lights on in Taylor's rooms. The eight houses in Alvarado Court, known locally as bungalows, were grouped in a U around a central garden landscaped with palmettos and shrubs and decorated with white-columned pergolas, flower urns, and stone seats. Three houses on either side faced across the U,

Taylor seated at the desk before which his murdered body was found.

Mabel Normand around the time she first met William Desmond Taylor.

with two houses at the closed east end. All eight were built of white stucco in a pseudo-Spanish style, with red-tiled roofs. Each house contained adjoining duplex apartments, with living room, dining room, and kitchen downstairs and bedrooms, bath, and closets upstairs. Alvarado Court, part of the then fashionable West Lake Park district of Hollywood, was located at the corner of Alvarado and Maryland streets.

The sixteen tenants of this rather smart enclave included such movie people as Agnes Ayres, famous for having starred with Rudolph Valentino in *The Sheik*; Douglas MacLean, who had acted in two films with Mary Pickford, *Johanna Enlists* (1918) and *Captain Kidd Jr.* (1919), both of which were directed by Taylor; Charles Maigne, who had directed Alice Brady, Irene Castle, and Mary Miles Minter in Paramount movies (he lived next to Taylor, in 404-A); and Edna Purviance, whose apartment, in the next house to the west, was 402-B. Taylor's apartment was 404-B. Known to his friends as Bill, William Desmond Taylor was not only a leading director, entitled to have his name above the titles of his films at Paramount–Famous Players–Lasky, but for five years his colleagues had chosen him as president of the seven-year-old Motion Picture Directors Association.

Blond and beautiful Edna Purviance had been discovered in San Francisco by Charlie Chaplin in 1915, after his departure from Keystone Comedies, where he had played opposite Mabel Normand. In need of a feminine foil for his tramp, he found her in Edna, whose soft beauty graced the Essanay and Mutual two-reelers and popular features like *Shoulder Arms* and *The Kid*. (Purviance remained on Chaplin's payroll until her death. Her only role as a star in her own right was in *A Woman of Paris*, with Adolphe Menjou playing her rich lover. Directed by Chaplin, who appeared in it briefly as a railway porter, it was a box-office disappointment, but its sophisticated style and décor had an important influence on later films.)

In the courtyard, Purviance, who had stopped momentarily when she saw Taylor's lighted rooms, decided not to ring his doorbell at that late hour and went to bed. Perhaps it was just as well. On the floor of the brightly lit room, in front of his desk, above which a photo of Mabel Normand hung, lay William Desmond Taylor's dead body.

Around seven-thirty the next morning, Purviance and others were awakened by the sounds coming from the courtyard. Henry Peavey, Taylor's black valet and cook, had arrived at his usual time to prepare his employer's breakfast. He had picked up the morning paper from the front porch and had brought some milk of magnesia Taylor had asked him to obtain at the druggist's for his nervous stomach. Peavey, puzzled that only the downstairs lights were lit, while the bedroom lights upstairs were dark so early in the morning, used his key to open the locked front door.

"The first thing I saw was his feet," he testified at the coroner's inquest. "I looked at his feet a few minutes and said, 'Mr. Taylor.' He never moved. I stepped a little further in the door, and seen his face, and turned and ran out and hollered." In a panic, Peavey stood in the courtyard, yelling, "Mr. Taylor's dead! Help, help! Mr. Taylor's dead!"

The first person to respond was E. C. Jessurun, the owner and manager of the court, who lived in the house just east of Taylor's, also occupied by the MacLeans. He

7

was followed by Charles Maigne and by Douglas Mac-Lean, who was wearing a dressing gown. When they entered Taylor's bungalow, the director lay on his back, head to the east and feet to the west, one arm at his side and the other outstretched. He was fully clothed, in vest, coat, collar, and tie. Crusted blood was visible around his mouth, but there was no sign of violence, except a slightly crumpled rug. "It looked like he had kicked it with his foot," Peavey said.

Douglas MacLean, describing Taylor's appearance, said: "He looked just like a dummy in a department store window, so perfect and immaculate. I was impressed with the fact that he looked like a wax figure dressed up." Peavey noticed that Taylor was wearing the same clothes as on the previous evening. This was unusual. Taylor, who dressed elegantly in the style of an English gentleman, owned an extensive wardrobe and changed it frequently.

While Jessurun used Taylor's phone to notify the police, several people in the courtyard entered or peered into the room, including Faith MacLean and her maid, Christine Jewett; and residents like Verne Dumas, a wealthy oilman; Mrs. E. C. Reddick, Neil Harrington, and Edna Purviance. No one knew the cause of Taylor's death, and everyone assumed it was from natural causes.

Taylor's chauffeur, Howard Fellows, arrived to drive his boss to the studio after breakfast and was stunned at the news. A little after eight-fifteen on the previous night, when he had put Taylor's car in the garage, he had seen the house lights lit and had rung the doorbell, intending to leave the car keys for Taylor, as instructed. Getting no response, he went home, where he phoned Taylor, without success.

He now phoned his brother, Harold Fellows. Harry, the director's previous chauffeur, had been taken on at Paramount by Taylor and had recently been promoted to assistant director. Harry immediately roused Charles Eyton, the studio's general manager, at his home.

Eyton acted quickly and illegally, in Paramount's interests. Apparently he, too, assumed Taylor's death was natural. He instructed Harry Fellows to rush to Taylor's house with Julia Crawford Ivers, the director's closest associate and Paramount's chief scenarist, and her son James Van Trees, who was Taylor's cameraman. Eyton knew they could reach Alvarado Court well ahead of him, and he urged them to get there before the police. They were to remove any items, such as liquor (since it was the Prohibition era) or letters, that might cause scandal or harm Taylor's reputation if revealed in the newspapers. As it happened, the Paramount trio had less than twenty minutes in which to act—between 7:40 and 7:58 a.m.

Detective Sergeant Thomas H. Ziegler, accompanied by a Los Angeles policeman, arrived at the scene from the Wilshire police station just before 8:00 a.m. As he drove up, Mrs. Ivers and her son sped off with Taylor's bootleg liquor. They had also taken letters that actresses Mary Miles Minter, Neva Gerber, and Mabel Normand had written him, as well as letters from Taylor's twenty-year-old daughter, Ethel Daisy, who lived in Mamaroneck, New York. (If there were other items, Eyton did not report them in his subsequent confrontation with District Attorney Thomas Lee Woolwine.) Harry Fellows remained at the scene, awaiting Eyton's arrival.

Ziegler's first action was to clear Taylor's rooms of people. Then he took statements from Peavey, Jessurun, the MacLeans, and a few others. Douglas MacLean said he and his wife thought they had heard a shot the night before. At this point, a doctor who happened to be visiting a patient nearby asked if he could examine the body. He started to turn the body over, but Ziegler stopped him and said they must await the coroner, who was on his way. After a cursory look, the doctor announced the cause of Taylor's death to be hemorrhage of the stomach, and Ziegler wrote "Natural Causes" on his report. The doctor (no one recorded his name) departed, never to be heard from again.

On learning of this medical verdict, Edna Purviance phoned Mabel Normand at her home. Mabel was shattered by the news of Taylor's sudden death and became hysterical.

On Charles Eyton's arrival, Ziegler treated this important studio executive with deference, making no attempt to stop him or accompany him when he went upstairs to the bedroom. Ziegler continued his questioning of the various residents.

When Eyton came downstairs, he was not asked about his movements or whether he had removed anything. He had in fact found a few letters missed by his colleagues, which he later acknowledged frankly—not at the inquest, where he was not asked about it—saying, "I simply wanted to protect innocent parties, including Taylor, from scandal." A rumor started by Hearst reporter Adela Rogers St. Johns that Eyton had burned papers in Taylor's fireplace was untrue. There was no fireplace in the house.

Around eight-forty, the deputy coroner, William Macdonald, arrived with his assistant and their truck. The cause of Taylor's death was finally revealed. Eyton, who assumed he had the right to interfere with police business, helped Macdonald turn the body over. There was blood on the carpet from a bullet wound on the left side of Taylor's back. The bullet had pierced the chest and lodged in Taylor's neck. It was the work of an expert gunman. Eyton exclaimed, "Good God, he's been murdered. Someone shot him in the back!" The postmortem examination would reveal a .38 caliber steel-nosed bullet.

The news shocked everyone. Faith MacLean, remembering her experience of the previous night, exclaimed, "So it *was* a gun shot!" at which Jessurun said, "Did you hear that too? I thought it might be a shot, but when nothing happened I decided I was mistaken. It was around eight o'clock when I heard it." But Faith MacLean realized that something very important had happened: not only had she heard the shot; she had seen the murderer.

On the previous evening, the MacLeans had finished dinner around 7:45 p.m. and their maid was clearing up. A half hour earlier, Christine had heard someone moving around in the alley between the MacLeans' house and Taylor's. "Mr. MacLean came home about five minutes past seven," she told reporters. "He honked his car horn to notify me he was ready for dinner. He then came into the house. I served the first course and then went out on the screened porch. When I had first heard the man, he was walking in the alley. Suddenly he stopped and stood still for a long time. I listened, fearing auto thieves. Then Mrs. MacLean rang the bell, and I had to go back to the dining room. When I finished serving the second course, I returned to the porch. The man was moving around; I heard his shoes scrape on the pavement. At intervals he would move and stand still."

The February evening had become unusually chilly for Hollywood. There was a snowstorm in the surrounding

Newspaper photo of Alvarado Court in 1922. Arrow points to Taylor bungalow.

The Taylor-MacLean corner of the courtyard, taken in the late 1920s.

San Bernardino mountains, where King Vidor and his company of actors were caught in a blizzard. Five or ten minutes before 8:00 p.m., Douglas MacLean had gone upstairs, looking for the portable electric heater. His wife had taken up her knitting and was seated on the living room sofa, when they heard what sounded like the report of a gun. (This was the sound that Mr. Jessurun, in the apartment adjoining theirs, also heard.)

The maid exclaimed, "Oh, wasn't that a shot?" but Faith said she thought it might have been a car backfiring. When Christine insisted, "I'm *sure* it was a shot," Faith put aside her knitting, went to her front door, and opened it. Newspapers described the MacLean apartment as "across from Taylor's," leading to the mistaken conclusion it was across the courtyard. It was in fact situated catercornered to Taylor's, at the closed eastern end of Alvarado Court, much nearer to where the murder was committed than was the house on the other side of the central garden.

As Faith MacLean looked at the lighted doorway of Taylor's house, she saw a stranger emerge. When the district attorney questioned her some time later (the coroner ignored her at the inquest), he asked, "Did he [the stranger] seem in a hurry?"

"No," she replied, "he was the coolest thing I have ever seen. He was facing Alvarado Street [away from her], and as I opened my door, I saw him. He turned around *and looked at me*—and hesitated. Then it seemed to me that Mr. Taylor must have spoken to him from inside the house. Seemed like he [the stranger] pulled the door shut. He turned around and, looking at me all the time, went down the couple of steps that go to Taylor's house. I thought it was just nothing, none of my business.

13

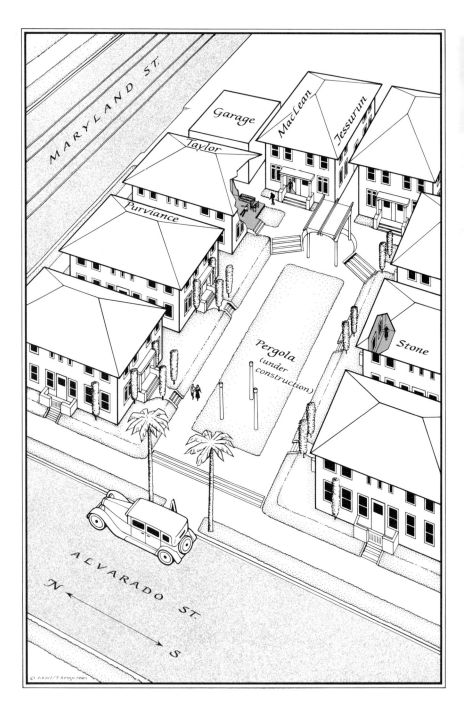

Maryland St.

Garage

MacLean

Jessurun

Taylor

Purviance

Pergola
(under
construction)

Stone

Alvarado St.

N

S

14

A police photograph of the objects found on Taylor—watch, locket, penknife, etc.

Interior of the living room, with body drawn in by newspaper artist.

I closed the door as he started in between the two houses [Taylor's and hers]. He went toward the alley and Maryland Street."

In other words, the stranger walked toward her, instead of turning to his right and leaving by Alvarado Street. When she was asked what he looked like, she said, "Well, he was—I don't know—sort of a roughly dressed man." Then she added, "He was dressed like my idea of a motion picture burglar." She was certain his suit was dark; he wore neither topcoat nor raincoat. She guessed his height to be about five feet nine and his weight to be one hundred seventy pounds. He had on a cap ("gray plaid," she thought) and either wore a muffler around his neck or had his jacket collar turned up, she was not sure which. She could not see his face distinctly, but she was certain it was smooth-shaven. Her phrase "sort of a roughly dressed man" suggests a decidedly masculine figure. He seemed neither surprised nor startled on seeing her, nor did he display the slightest sign of alarm—a cool customer indeed. All this convinced her the maid had been mistaken about the shot. She even thought the stranger may have smiled at her; at least his lips had opened in a sort of upward curl. She was so certain it was an auto backfire she had heard that when her husband came downstairs with the heater, she didn't think it worthwhile telling him what she had seen in Taylor's doorway.

She now told Douglas MacLean what she had witnessed the previous night, and he asked her the question that was to be repeated over and over again by everyone investigating the crime: "Do you think it was Sands?"

He was referring to the enigmatic Edward F. Sands, Taylor's former cook, valet, and secretary, who had absconded in the summer of 1921, during the director's absence in England, after forging and cashing checks for more than five thousand dollars, wrecking his employer's car, and stealing his jewelry and clothes. Faith MacLean, who knew the chubby young man well and had often seen Sands wearing his floppy cook's hat when preparing food for Taylor, was certain the stranger was *not* Sands. Asked if the chauffeur Howard Fellows, whom she also knew, could have been the man, she said it was not Fellows. It was a stranger. Besides, Fellows had said he rang the doorbell after 8:15 p.m., and she saw the stranger around 8:00 p.m.

Though the stranger, according to Faith MacLean, resembled a movie burglar, nothing had been taken from the house. Left behind were Taylor's wallet, containing seventy-eight dollars; a two-carat diamond ring; a silver cigarette case, a Christmas gift from Mabel Normand; an ivory toothpick; and a platinum Waltham pocket watch, whose winding mechanism—according to the police—had run down at 7:19 a.m., just before Peavey's arrival. Taylor's watch chain held a silver pencil, a metal stamp used to validate checks, a penknife, and a nail clipper. Taylor was also wearing a wristwatch, newly fashionable and socially acceptable for men through widespread use by the military in the war (Taylor had been a captain in the Canadian Army). His coat pockets contained a half-used packet of cough drops, a linen handkerchief, and a silver locket with a photograph of Mabel Normand.

Coroner Macdonald, busy with his medical examination of the corpse, was joined by Eyton, who officiously insisted on helping him to open Taylor's clothes. They found an enormous bloodstain on the left side of his shirt. After Taylor's vest and coat were removed, the bullet hole in the back of the coat was found to be lower than the corresponding hole in the vest. Taylor must have had his arms raised in the air when he was shot.

There were three words—"To My Dearest"—engraved beneath the photo of Mabel Normand that Taylor kept in the silver locket. These words, reported in the press, would have been painful reading for Mary Miles Minter, one of Paramount's biggest stars; she had done everything in her power to replace Mabel in Taylor's affection from the moment she met him. Their first meeting had occurred three years earlier, when Taylor was assigned to direct one of her most successful movies, *Anne of Green Gables.*

"I knew when I laid eyes on him," Mary asserted, "that he was the only man in the world for me." She added, "He reciprocated my love," but this was wishful thinking. Taylor told male friends that he was flattered by Mary's infatuation (she was the same age as his daughter, Ethel Daisy) but her behavior had become a source of worry for him. She wanted a promise of marriage, but he refused, reminding her that her million-dollar Paramount contract, which expired in 1923, would become invalid if she broke the "no marriage" clause. Not only was she a minor, with whom he had to keep on good terms professionally, but her suspicious mother, Charlotte Shelby, was reputedly dangerous to tangle with. Mary did not learn of Taylor's murder—and it was her mother she learned it from—until 11 a.m. on the morning his body was discovered. She rushed at once to Alvarado Court, but he had already been taken to the mortuary.

Between eight-thirty and ten o'clock that morning, the courtyard was crowded with reporters from the seven Los Angeles daily newspapers and from out-of-town papers, together with wire-service newsmen and the inevitable

The detectives and other Taylor case officials, unable (or not allowed) to solve the murder, pose before his house. From left: Deputy County Surveyor Heuer, Detective Sgt. Winn, Deputy D.A. Doran, Detective Sgt. Cline, Deputy County Surveyors Timmons and Atkins, Investigator Contreras of the D.A.'s office, and Detective Sgt. Murphy, photographed on February 3, 1922.

press photographers. They all knew that this was a "big story," destined to dominate front pages with headlines for many weeks. When the newsmen learned that Mabel Normand was the last person to have seen William Desmond Taylor alive, they made a dash for her house.

2

The Director's Last Night

$\mathbf{M}$ABEL NORMAND was sitting at her bedroom dressing table, crying. She was trying to make herself up for *Suzanna*, a story of old California, which was being filmed by Mack Sennett at First National. The studio limousine was waiting to take her to location for the day's work, for which she had donned her Spanish costume, including a large sombrero. The news of Taylor's murder, which Edna Purviance had confirmed by phone, was so shattering that she was unprepared to cope with the horde of newsmen now at her door.

"There was a ringing at my doorbell and a clamor outside," she told an interviewer. "The wildest mob I ever saw tumbled into my living room—detectives and reporters and press photographers and curious strangers. They hurled a million questions. Then it dawned on me that it might be in the minds of some of them that I had murdered my friend! That ghastly possibility made me frantic. I imagine that the more I talked, the less sense

I made about a perfectly innocent coincidence—I happen to have been the last person who saw Taylor alive, except for his murderer."

Over and over again, starting with the inquest and for the eight years until her death in 1930, Mabel recounted to reporters and other writers her part in the events of Taylor's last night. In later versions (and her words are taken from several different accounts), her language became a bit more self-conscious, but the given facts were always consistent. No one thought she was guilty of Taylor's murder, yet she seemed guilt-ridden. At the same time she claimed in interviews that things had been looking bright for her at the start of 1922:

"Late in January we began to make *Suzanna*. The whole world and my future seemed cheerful and promising. Not only was my new picture a good one, but I felt that at last I was coming into my own as a comedienne. And my friendship with Bill Taylor was one of the finest things in my life. He was a splendid director, and we often went together to see the new movies. It was because of his counsel in the matter of books that I saw him on the last day of his life."

Mack Sennett had given her that day off, saying he would notify her if she was needed on the set the following day. On February 1, she awoke around noon and dawdled about the house. Mamie Owens, the motherly black woman who was her housekeeper, dresser, and devoted servant, served her a late lunch. Mabel decided to spend an hour or so downtown, exchanging duplicate Christmas presents she'd done nothing about for five weeks. She also thought it was high time to return her most valuable jewels, taken out for holiday parties, to the safety vaults of Hellman's Night and Day Bank. By the time her chauf-

Mabel Normand, with Mamie Owens combing her hair.

feur, William Davis, drove her downtown, it was nearly five o'clock.

"As I left the house," she said, "I took my volume of Freud [*The Interpretation of Dreams*], which Taylor had told me to read." He encouraged her to read serious books and to brush up on her French (her background was French-Canadian on her father's side, Irish-American on her mother's). On completing her errands, she saw that Harold Lloyd's new movie, *A Sailor-Made Man*, had just opened, and she phoned Mamie Owens not to expect her for dinner. But Mamie said, "You can't go to the picture tonight, because Mr. Sennett called and said for you to be ready to go on location tomorrow, with your makeup on. And Mr. Taylor just phoned and said he had two books for you. He wanted to know if he should bring them here, or would you call for them. You ought to drive by his place and get the books, and then come on home. I'll serve your dinner in bed, and comb your hair, so you can get up bright and early for work." Since it was now nearly seven o'clock, Mabel agreed to do as Mamie suggested.

"I wondered what books Bill had bought for me," Mabel stated. "I had my Freud with me, and I thought he'd be pleased to know I had read in it in my car." She spotted a peanut stand at one corner and stopped to buy several bags of roasted unshelled nuts. She also bought the *Police Gazette*, because the studio publicity staff required some new stills for *Suzanna* and she saw possibilities in their cover girl's pose. When her car arrived at Alvarado Court, which it could not enter, she told Davis to wait for her and to clean out the peanut shells scattered on the floor.

> One of Taylor's peculiarities [she explained] is that he never closed his front door during the day,

and seldom at night. When I rang his bell, Henry Peavey came to the door and I heard Bill inside, talking on the telephone. His rooms were small and I said I would wait outside until he finished. Soon after Henry told him I was there, he said goodbye to the caller and came to the door smiling, and held out both hands. "Hello, Mabel darling," he said, "I know what you've come for—the two books." "Righto, my bright duck," I said, going in, "and I've brought you a present. Guess what it is." I held the bag of peanuts behind my back.

"No man could possibly guess what you'd buy, but I'll bet it's something nice," he said. "Come on in and have some dinner. I'm finishing, but Peavey can fix you something."

"No, Mamie's going to feed me in bed tonight. I'm working on location tomorrow and have to retire early." I could see through the arch that separated the two downstairs rooms that the table was covered with dishes. I said, "Why don't you finish your dinner?" He said, "I don't want dessert, but you'll have a cocktail with me, won't you?" "Sure," I said. "And I've got just the thing for your dessert, Bill, a bag of peanuts." He laughed and put the bag on top of his piano. They found it there, untouched, the next morning. Then he shouted to Peavey to mix a couple of cocktails, and sat down in front of his desk, which was covered with cancelled checks.

Taylor had been going over his checkbook and other accounts in preparation for his income tax report, due (in that era) on March 15. Mabel said the person he had been talking to on the phone, while she waited outside, was his financial adviser, Marjorie Berger, who had many

Looking from Taylor's living room into the dining room, with the kitchen beyond at right.

movie people (including Mabel) as clients and whose office Taylor had visited earlier that day. It was learned that around seven o'clock he had phoned his friend Antonio Moreno, an actor who needed advice about his career; they were to meet the next day.

Pointing at the checks, Taylor told Mabel that many of them had been forged by Edward Sands. Picking up one check he knew he had signed himself, Taylor held it next to others. "Neither of us," said Mabel, "could see any difference in the signatures." When Mabel asked

Henry Peavey, Taylor's cook.

Taylor what he was going to do about Sands, he replied, "What on earth can I do? He's been missing since my return [from Europe the previous July]. I'm afraid I'll never get it straightened out."

Henry Peavey, wearing his butler's white coat, came in with the cocktails he had mixed—Orange Blossoms (gin and orange juice), the new postwar rage. He set down a tray with a tall cocktail shaker and glasses, which the police found on the table next morning. Taylor told Peavey he could go as soon as he had cleared away the dinner things. Peavey hurried to finish in the kitchen, went upstairs to change, and came down wearing green golf stockings, yellow plus fours, and a purple tie. "He was so funny," Mabel recalled. "I don't know why he was wearing golf clothes at night, but I said to Bill, 'If you'd let him play golf more often, he wouldn't get in any more trouble in the park.' " Knowing that Peavey was homosexual, she was slyly referring to his arrest for vagrancy and for alleged indecent exposure in West Lake Park. Taylor had put up bail of two hundred dollars and had promised to appear in court on Peavey's behalf on February 2.

After Peavey left, Taylor took from a shelf the books he had bought for Mabel and unwrapped them—a novel by Ethel M. Dell, entitled *Rosa Mundi*, which he thought might be adapted for a Mabel Normand movie, and a translation from the German of a book about Nietzsche. "Together we turned the pages," said Mabel, "as people will with a new book." She also said they discussed a new novel, *Three Soldiers*, "by that Chicago newspaperman, John Dos Passos." Taylor asked about Mabel's progress with her new film, *Suzanna*, and she wanted to know about the movie Taylor had recently completed, *The Green Temptation*, with Betty Compson and Theodore Kosloff. They also made a date to see the Harold Lloyd movie and perhaps go out for dinner. When Mabel reminded Taylor that her car was waiting at the curb, he said he would phone her again at 9 p.m., but she warned him that Mamie would not disturb her after she retired.

Meanwhile the man whose movements the MacLeans' maid had heard in the alleyway stood waiting behind or beside Taylor's house for his chance to confront the director alone.

William Davis, Normand's chauffeur.

Bill walked down to the street with me [Mabel concluded] and laughed when he saw the peanut shells Davis had swept out of the car. There was the *Police Gazette* lying beside my Freud book, and he said, "Who else in this world could straddle two such extremes? Mabel, my darling, I'm afraid you're hopeless! Sometimes I wonder what's to become of you, my dear. Oh Mabel, what a lovely thing it would be if perfect love and trust could come into your strange life." He looked at me and shook his head, for he loved me dearly. I pulled his ear lobe and said, "Don't be silly, Bill. You won't believe it, but I bought that *Police Gazette* for the cover girl's pose." He helped me into the car and Davis started to drive away. I looked back and we wafted kisses on our hands as long as I could see him. I even kissed the window and left a little lipstick on it, which detectives found later.

I never saw Bill again. He did not telephone at nine as he promised. He was shot in the back when he reached his rooms a few minutes after I left him. The next morning, all hell broke loose. It raged about my head for weeks, identifying me with a crime I had no more to do with than you did.

Mabel's statement is an interesting psychological document, with its insistence on books and culture as the basis for their friendship, even as their behavior reveals that Taylor was in love and Mabel was responsive. There is no reason to believe that their last meeting differed in any detail from what she tells us. It is what she does not tell, and realizes she cannot tell, that is important: it would have meant The End for her career.

3

The Producers' Crisis

By 1920, Hollywood was established as the capital of a fantastically successful entertainment industry. Following the primitive nickelodeon era, the turning point or great leap forward of the movies occurred in January 1915, with the release of D. W. Griffith's *The Birth of a Nation*—the first American feature film of twelve reels and the first movie to gross millions of dollars. When European studios had to cut back early in the war, before the U.S. involvement in 1917, American films came to dominate the market. As Anita Loos put it, "World War One was *the* reason for Hollywood."

After the November 1918 Armistice, Hollywood boomed. Between 1910 and 1920, its population rose 720 percent. It became a crowded mecca for young aspirants to fame and fortune. Gloria Swanson, who progressed from Keystone Comedies to being a DeMille star, wrote from her own experience: "Fame was thrilling only until it became grueling. Money was fun only until you ran out of things to buy. Hollywood abounded with the victims of both—driven creatures, endlessly looking for solace or compensation in alcohol, drugs, and sex."* Nationally this was the start of an era of big crime in bootleg liquor and hard drugs, financed by big money. Locally the English author Aleister Crowley, who visited Hollywood at this time, described the residents as "the cinema crowd of cocaine-crazed sexual lunatics."

Cocaine, hailed as a wonder drug in the late nineteenth century, was long available without prescription and was not outlawed until 1914, when the Harrison Act was passed. In 1916, Douglas Fairbanks made a comedy about drug addiction for Triangle, *The Mystery of the Leaping Fish*, in which he played a detective-addict named Coke Ennyday. In 1903, the new drink Coca-Cola had been advertised as "exhilarating, invigorating, containing the tonic properties of the wonderful coca plant and the famous cola nut, on draught at soda fountains at five cents a glass." The traffic in hard drugs and the sale and use of narcotics reached unprecedented levels before and during the war years, 1914–18, according to the Federal Bureau of Narcotics.

It is not widely known that the number of persons addicted, in proportion to the population of the United States, was much higher in 1914 than in the 1950s. There were 200,000 addicts in 1914 (one out of every 400 persons), while in 1957 there were 45,000 addicts (one out of every 3,500 persons). This graph, prepared in 1961 by the U.S. Commissioner of Narcotics, Harry J. Anslinger,† shows there was a great drop after 1922, while

---

* Gloria Swanson, *Swanson on Swanson* (New York: Random House, 1980), p. 214.

† Harry J. Anslinger, *The Murderers: The Story of the Narcotic Gangs* (New York: Farrar, Straus & Giroux, 1961), app. 2.

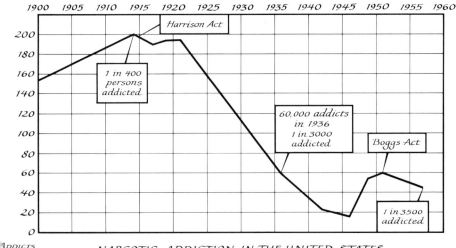

NARCOTIC ADDICTION IN THE UNITED STATES

addiction rose again in 1946, following the end of World War II (and of course went much higher after 1960).

According to Gertrude Jobes,* the biggest "central bank and clearing-house for the world's illicit trade in opium, morphine, cocaine and heroin ever organized up to that time" was run in California in 1920 by the Elie Heliopulos family. This Greek name means "sun god," and at least one member of the family cleverly changed his name to Godsol. Among the most famous drug addicts in Hollywood in the 1920s were Juanita Hansen, Barbara La Marr, Mabel Normand, Jack Pickford, Wallace Reid, Alma Rubens, and Olive Thomas. (Scores of less famous actors got busted, of course, but few readers paid much attention to obscure names. For example, when the *New York Times* listed actresses "Birdie Green, Paulette La-

* Gertrude Jobes, *Motion Picture Empire* (Hamden, Conn.: Archon Books, 1966), p. 177.

Fargue, May Hoffman, Minnie Leder and Lillian Miller"
—all of whom admitted they had heroin in their purses
—scarcely anyone remembered them; they were not
stars.) *Vanity Fair* in 1922 ran a satirical piece captioned
"Happy Days in Hollywood":

> With the brightening influence of Spring, there has
> been a distinct quickening of the social pace. Drugs
> are not as much in evidence as during the more trying
> days of winter, but they still spread their genial in-
> fluence at some of the more exclusive functions. Last
> week little Lulu Lenore of the Cuckoo Comedy Com-
> pany gave a small house dance for the younger ad-
> dicts. "Will you come to my 'Snow'-ball?" read the
> clever invitations. In one corner of the living-room
> was a miniature "Drug-store," where [a man] kept
> the company in a roar as he dispensed little pack-
> ages of cocaine, morphine and heroin. The guests
> at their departure received exquisite hypodermic
> needles in vanity boxes which have caused many
> heart-burnings among those who were not invited.

Hollywood was able to keep things quiet until a series
of sex and drug scandals occurred that nothing could cover
up. The first incident to get international coverage was
the death in Paris of beautiful Olive Thomas, who was
married to Jack Pickford. After she died from a drug
overdose, her name was found on the list of clients of a
U.S. Army officer busted for dealing in large quantities
of heroin and cocaine. Newspaper readers were shocked;
the popular American term for drug addicts was "dope
fiends."

By the time of William Desmond Taylor's murder, early in 1922, Hollywood was facing a crisis so serious that the highly competitive movie moguls closed ranks in a rare show of unity. Three major events contributed to the crisis: (1) the sensational sex scandal of the Fatty Arbuckle case; (2) the revelation that the actor Wallace Reid, a model of all-American manhood, had died as a result of drug addiction; and (3) Taylor's mysterious murder. As the film historian William K. Everson wrote: "The three coming together, and at a time when Hollywood was already being criticized for the sexual and other 'objectionable' content in films as diverse as *Foolish Wives* and *The Sheik*, posed a real threat."*

Public outrage over the Arbuckle scandal dominated the headlines for four months between September 1921 and January 1922, and the studio executives were badly frightened. According to Terry Ramsaye, by December 1921, "the motion picture men were sinking deeper and deeper into the gloom of the industry's disgrace. They needed a friend, quickly." Alarmed at the possibility of boycotts and national censorship, the moguls—Adolph Zukor, Marcus Loew, Winfield Sheehan, William Fox, Courtland Smith, Samuel Goldwyn, Carl Laemmle, R. H. Cochrane, Lewis J. Selznick, and others—finally took action.

To head the new Motion Picture Producers and Distributors Association, they hired former postmaster general Will Hays, a member of President Warren Harding's cabinet and chairman of the Republican National Com-

* William K. Everson, *American Silent Film* (New York: Oxford University Press, 1978), p. 296.

mittee, to institute controls and act as a morals czar, at a salary of $100,000 a year, greater than that of the President himself. Senator Henry L. Myers of Montana, a Presbyterian pillar of society (he was also a Mason, a Knight of Pythias, and an Elk), then gave Hollywood the fright of its life by drafting a bill for federal regulation of the movie industry. One of Hays's earliest priorities was to use his Washington connections to block the Myers bill from getting anywhere in Congress.

Director King Vidor has described the climate: "The movie bosses just didn't know which way to turn. Louis B. Mayer said to me, 'If this pressure keeps up, there won't be any more film business.' I think one of Hays' jobs was to keep them from pursuing the [Taylor] case. They were anxious to suppress the whole thing. They'd rather sacrifice Taylor than sacrifice the whole industry."*

According to actor Conrad Nagel, "Reform groups started referring to Hollywood as Sodom and Gomorrah. . . . They had 25 state legislatures considering 25 censorship bills, which would have ruined Hollywood."† Film producer Walter Wanger was candid about Hollywood's inevitable reaction to the crisis and the kind of action it resorted to: "Censorship trouble was precipitated by the Fatty Arbuckle case and with Wally Reid, a tremendous star, who used to take dope. . . . *Sometimes a cover-up of the goings-on was necessary* [italics added]. Every studio had a police department. . . . If a star was picked up drunk, influence could be exerted with politicians to keep his name clean."‡

* Kevin Brownlow, *Hollywood: The Pioneers* (New York: Alfred A. Knopf, 1979), p. 112.

† Bernard Rosenberg and Harry Silverstein, eds., *The Real Tinsel* (New York: Macmillan, 1970), p. 179.

‡ Ibid., p. 90.

The unfortunate Fatty Arbuckle is at the center of perhaps the biggest Hollywood myth. For years he had been a popular comedian at Mack Sennett's studio, featured as one of the famous Keystone Kops and later starred with Mabel Normand in a series of comedies, before moving to Paramount. According to the myth, twenty-five-year-old actress Virginia Rappe (she pronounced it Rappay) died after being raped by Arbuckle at the wild party he threw in a San Francisco hotel over Labor Day weekend in 1921. Reporters alleged that Virginia's bladder was fatally ruptured by a combination of Arbuckle's weight (266 pounds) and a Coca-Cola (or champagne) bottle with which he abused her. "The evidence was considered so vile, so unspeakable," wrote Gloria Swanson, "that much of it was passed around silently, in type-written notes."* Mabel Normand, who had been invited to the party by Arbuckle, was fortunately unable to attend.

The public reaction to the lurid newspaper stories was hysterical. Headlines read: TORTURE OF VIRGINIA RAPPE CHARGED (*San Francisco Examiner*); ICE ON ACTRESS BIG JOKE TO ARBUCKLE (*Los Angeles Examiner*); ARBUCKLE DRAGGED RAPPE GIRL TO ROOM, WOMAN TESTIFIES (*New York Times*); ARBUCKLE BAN DEMANDED BY MOTHERS' CONGRESS (*Chicago Tribune*). A Women's Vigilant Committee of San Francisco, headed by Dr. Mariana Bertola, was formed to see that justice was done; its members haunted the courtrooms during Arbuckle's three trials. Jennie Partridge, president of the Federation of Women's Clubs, said: "It is a disgrace that any girl should have to suffer from this man's ruthlessness. Arbuckle should be

---

* *Swanson on Swanson*, p. 168.

Fatty and Mabel at Keystone in He Did and He Didn't.

made to suffer." In Hartford, Connecticut, another group of vigilante women ripped down the screen of a movie theater showing an Arbuckle comedy. Some cowboys in Thermopolis, Wyoming, shot up the screen of a movie house during an Arbuckle short. An editorial in the *San Francisco Examiner* was captioned: "Hollywood Must Stop Using San Francisco for a Garbage Can."

The truth did not surface until 1976: The doomed actress, a prostitute who came to the party pregnant, was in fact a victim of gonorrhea and an infected bladder, which caused her such severe pain that after some heavy drinking, she screamed and tore off her clothes until other drunken partygoers—except Arbuckle, who was in another room—dropped her into a bathtub full of ice "to relieve her pain." It was indeed a wild party. The further truth is that the doctors who attended her (she died in a *maternity* hospital the following Friday) apparently suppressed evidence of an abortion and faked their postmortem examination.

Arbuckle's worst crime was that he got beastly drunk on Prohibition liquor. He neither raped Virginia Rappe nor had any sexual contact with her nor abused her in any way. On the contrary, early that evening she had appealed to him for financial aid to pay for an abortion, and he promised her his help. He was framed by Maude Delmont, an older woman who brought Virginia to the party and decided to grasp the opportunity fate had put in her hands. It was she who initiated the charges against him, after wiring her attorney:

WE HAVE ROSCOE ARBUCKLE IN A HOLE HERE.

CHANCE TO MAKE SOME MONEY OUT OF HIM.

The prosecution, knowing she would be exposed as a liar, never allowed Delmont to be put on the stand. Arbuckle endured three trials, the first two juries being unable to agree on a verdict. The third jury exonerated him, and the foreman took the unusual course of reading out an apology for "the great injustice that has been done him."

Despite his acquittal, Arbuckle's career as an actor was finished. He was banned in April 1922 by the movie industry's new "friend," Will Hays. It seems strange that a *New York Times* editorial should have endorsed Hays's ban on the grounds that "Arbuckle has become, through mischance, a symbol of all the vice that has been indulged in by the movie people" and because, even though he was adjudged innocent, "an odor still clings to him." The odor continued to cling for decades, until all the facts, including court transcripts and records hitherto unavailable, were published.* Such was the power of the press that, in some quarters, the odor still clings. Arbuckle was permitted to direct a few films under another name. Always the comedian, he chose the name Will B. Goode, which Hays immediately changed to William Goodrich.

As for Wallace Reid, Cecil B. DeMille admitted that "the terrible shock of his death . . . almost shattered Hollywood." It was impossible for Will Hays to suppress the news of Reid's drug addiction. The young blond actor was a handsome, blue-eyed, charming, and immensely popular American idol, a good athlete who excelled at swimming and driving racing cars. He had a first-rate comic talent and he was also musical, good at the violin and piano. As a youth he attended the Freehold Military School in New Jersey, intending to go on to Princeton, but after his father, Hal Reid, a successful playwright, asked him to understudy the juvenile lead in his new play,

* David A. Yallop, *The Day the Laughter Stopped* (New York: St. Martin's Press, 1976).

he was destined for success as an actor. His brief appearance as a fighting blacksmith in *The Birth of a Nation* made him famous, and he became a star at twenty-three, opposite Lillian Gish in *Enoch Arden*. During World War I and in the postwar years he was the top male star at Paramount, appearing with Gloria Swanson in *The Affairs of Anatol*, with Geraldine Farrar in *Joan the Woman* and *Carmen*, with Bebe Daniels in *Nice People*, and with Agnes Ayres in Booth Tarkington's *Clarence*. Perhaps his most distinguished role was in the movie version of *Peter Ibbetson* with Elsie Ferguson (the film was called *Forever*).

"Behind that flashing facade of health and comeliness," wrote Laurence Stallings, "there was a shocking secret. Our hero was in the habit of dosing himself with morphine sulfate, just as much of the junk as he deemed necessary to keep going." Some claim the habit arose from a painful injury he suffered in an action film, *The Valley of the Giants*; a doctor had administered morphine so that Reid could complete the film, and he depended on opiates thereafter. Even if this was the actual beginning, his own deep-seated need and the prevalence of pushers may have contributed. In addition to the great pressures under which he worked, there was a self-critical and depressive side to his character. He felt he had never been in a movie worth its coat of silver oxide: "I do not like the parts I play. I'm no hero, I'm nothing. I have a race-car driver's license, but the studio is afraid I'll kill myself if I try for the Indianapolis speedway tests." He knew that he had no real life of his own; the studio owned him.

Reid feared the consequences when Adolph Zukor and Jesse Lasky, the heads of Paramount, would learn his secret, as they inevitably did owing to his increasingly

Mary Miles Minter before a Paramount poster for Wallace Reid's Double Speed

erratic behavior on the set. He had become thin and pale, delayed production by reporting late, and bumped into furniture. On one occasion, he sat on the floor and started to cry. Lasky in his memoirs* relates that Reid agreed to have a studio doctor live with him around the clock for ten days, to guarantee that he took no drugs. Verbally the doctor gave him a clean bill of health, but blood tests showed that Reid had taken drugs almost nightly. The doctor, new to the problem, was deceived by the traditional addict's cunning. Reid enjoyed outwitting the bosses, according to director James Cruze: "On the golf course I saw the syringe, needle and dope he concealed in a golf-club handle." Cruze described him as "a great big kid, and the sweetest guy I ever saw."

Reid's downfall was a major blow to millions of disillusioned fans. Only the baseball betrayal of the Chicago White Sox and the fall from heroism of Shoeless Joe Jackson surpassed the revelation that Wallace Reid, the all-American boy, was a dope fiend. Finally, he agreed to kick the habit at the Banksia Place Sanitarium. "He sent me a telegram," said Cecil B. DeMille, "assuring me he would be on hand for the starting date of our new picture. He had no notion of losing his fight." But the cure was worse than the illness. "Wally was cured," his widow, actress Dorothy Davenport, explained, "but terribly debilitated. Only a return to drugs under control could have saved him. He refused." The first setback to his drug-weakened system was hypostatic pneumonia, then his heart gave out. He died at thirty.

Will Hays had banned all references to dope and drug addiction on the screen, but because of the tremendous

* Jesse L. Lasky, *I Blow My Own Horn*, with Don Weldon (New York: Doubleday, 1957), p. 158.

newspaper coverage of Reid's illness and death, followed by the determination of Mrs. Reid to publicize it, Hays agreed that she could make a propaganda picture about the dangers of drug addiction. *Human Wreckage*, starring Bessie Love and Mrs. Wallace Reid and directed by John Griffith Wray, was released in 1923. It opened with this foreword:

> Dope is the gravest menace which today confronts the United States. Immense quantities of morphine, heroin and cocaine are yearly smuggled into America across the Canadian and Mexican borders. The Dope Ring is composed of rings within rings, the inner ring undoubtedly including men powerful in finance, politics and society. But the trail to the "men higher up" is cunningly covered. No investigator has penetrated to the inner circle.

When Will Hays published his memoirs, readers looking for light on the three great crises of 1922 got short shrift. His references to the scandals are minimal and oblique. He covers the Taylor and Arbuckle cases in one badly worded subordinate clause, stating that Hollywood in the pre–Hays Office days "had not judged, in the cases precipitated by the Arbuckle case and the William D. Taylor murder, that it was not equipped either to handle public relations on a national scale or to secure the unified effort needed toward industry self-regulation. Hence the Motion Picture Producers and Distributors Association was founded."*

Hays mentions Wallace Reid by name only once: "Plenty of people were only too willing to believe that stories like those of Fatty Arbuckle and Wally Reid were

* Will H. Hays, *Memoirs* (New York: Doubleday, 1955), p. 357.

typical." He manages to refer to Reid's addiction without using the star's name: "A story broke about a very real narcotics scandal involving a popular star." Though his book has an index, the names of Roscoe Arbuckle, Wallace Reid, and William Desmond Taylor do not appear in it. Mabel Normand and Mary Miles Minter are never named. Will Hays not only swept Hollywood's dirt under the rug, as he was paid to do, but thirty-three years later he was pretending the dirt hardly existed.

The newest Hollywood scandal, the Taylor murder case, was scandalous not because the murder was unsolved but because it was transformed by the newspapers into a sex case. Its central erotic symbol became Mary Miles Minter's pink panties (or was it actually her nightgown?), monogrammed with the initials MMM. These were equivalent to Fatty Arbuckle's Coca-Cola (or was it champagne?) bottle. As with the Arbuckle bottle, no one ever saw the panties/nightgown, or even a photograph of them, because they did not exist. This symbol was the invention of star newspaper reporters like Adela Rogers St. Johns, a leading "sob sister" (as they were called) for William Randolph Hearst.

Mary Miles Minter adored Taylor, yearned to be his mistress, and tried unsuccessfully to stay with him overnight. She would have been elated—as she was when she learned he had kept a letter of hers—to know that he treasured an article of her clothing, yet to her dying day she swore that the pink panties never existed. A few years before she died, at age eighty-four, she reiterated in a phone interview with the film historian Kevin Brownlow that Adela Rogers St. Johns lied when "she claimed she once held in her hands the famous pink panties—after that, it grew to be a nightgown—embroidered with butterflies and the initials MMM." As she told Brownlow: "So much hogwash has been written to make money. . . . Well, my mother bought my undergarments and I can just imagine her having my initials embroidered! And yet I have read of this thing for years—Mary Miles Minter's famous pink nightgown. I marvel to this day where it arose. . . . What they *did* find was my handkerchief. One time I had something in my eye, and Mr. Taylor said, 'Here, take a real handkerchief, not that little dab of lace.' " They exchanged handkerchiefs, and hers "was found at his desk. . . . As for underwear, it's a joke, laughable and pathetic," she said.*

Over the years, she offered a reward of one thousand dollars, never claimed, to anyone who could produce the highly publicized garment. Many years later, the police files were examined by a friend of hers, a retired police official, and no clothing of hers, except for the handkerchief, was found in the archives. But the pink panties or flimsy nightgown seized the imagination of newspaper readers and stayed in the headlines and news columns for months.

A possible source for the monogram and the butterfly might have been Mary's love letter to Taylor, which Charles Eyton and his colleagues overlooked in their hurried search of the rooms the morning his murder was discovered. When the police subsequently gave Taylor's shelves and furniture a systematic going-over, a letter fell out of one of his books. Written in a childish scrawl on scented paper, with the initial M drawn as part of a butterfly monogram decoration, it said:

* Brownlow, *Hollywood*, p. 111.

> Dearest—
>   I love you—I love you—
> I love you———x x x x x x x x x
>   X
>   Yours always!
>   Mary

The final X was enormous. This letter was widely depicted and the newspapers also reproduced Mary's inscription to Taylor on a large photo of herself: "For William Desmond Taylor, artist, gentleman, Man! Sincere good wishes, Mary Miles Minter, 1920." It did not matter that the police also found photos inscribed to Taylor by Mary Pickford, Mabel Normand, and Winifred Kingston, an English actress. (The latter was Mrs. Dustin Farnum in private life; Taylor had directed Mr. and Mrs. Farnum at both Balboa and Pallas-Paramount studios.)

Mary's fervent declaration of love catapulted her into the national consciousness as a sex symbol. She had long been regarded as lovely to look at but virginal (and therefore not very good copy), which is what her mother, Charlotte Shelby, preferred. After Mary's retirement from the screen, when their intrafamily lawsuits over money were in the courts, her sister Margaret released to the press excerpts from Mary's private diary giving an account of her early love affair with actor James Kirkwood, their secret ritualistic marriage, and an alleged abortion.

In 1922, it was not Mary Miles Minter but William Desmond Taylor who was "exposed" by the press. He was denounced as the seducer of young women, an evil Don Juan who got what he deserved—a bullet in his back.

The butterfly monogram on Minter's love letter to Taylor.

Mary Miles Minter in front of her Hollywood home.

4

Taylor's Years of Struggle

THE MAN lying dead on the Alvarado Court bungalow floor was eleven weeks short of his fiftieth birthday, though in publicity releases he admitted to only forty-five years. In some of his last photos, he looked so haggard he could have been taken for sixty. At the end of a checkered and arduous life—mostly a struggle to earn money, beginning in his eighteenth year, when he had broken with his father—he had finally achieved financial success and attained a top reputation as a movie director, under an assumed name.

His real name was William Cunningham Deane-Tanner, and he was born into an upper-middle-class Anglo-Irish family from Cork, whose ranks included distinguished architects, doctors, government officials, and military officers. He had come a long way from his ancestral homes—The Elms, in Carlow, fifty-six miles southwest of Dublin, where he was born; the family estate, Belleville Park, in the village of Cappoquin in County

Waterford; and a large house at 3 Upper Merwin Street, Dublin. His father was a British Army officer, Major Kearns Deane-Tanner of the Carlow Rifles, a martinet who made his son's life miserable. William was born on April 26, 1872, the second of four children (Ellen, or Nellie, was a year older, Elizabeth Mary was born in 1874, and Denis, the youngest, in 1876).

His paternal grandfather, William Kearns Tanner, M.D., was a fellow of the Royal College of Surgeons of Ireland, who taught at Queen's University College, Cork, where he was professor of surgery for nearly twenty years. Dr. Tanner had three sons: Major Tanner, the father of William; Dr. Lombard Tanner, a physician who died in London; and Dr. Charles Deane Tanner, M.P., who represented mid-Cork in the House of Commons at Westminster from 1885 until his death in 1901. Dr. Charlie, as the M.P. was called, was an ardent Nationalist, pro-Parnell and pro–Irish Republic, whereas William's father, the major, was violently Unionist and pro-English. The third brother, Dr. Lombard, had committed suicide. After Taylor's murder, there were reports that the grandfather had died a violent death, but these stories were erroneous.

Taylor's paternal grandmother, née Elizabeth Deane, came from a somewhat higher social stratum than her husband. Her family's most illustrious figure was her father, Sir Thomas Deane (1792–1871), mayor of Cork in 1830 and a leading architect in his day. One of his most famous buildings was the addition he built "in Venetian style" to Trinity College, Dublin. It comes into Leopold Bloom's purview during his walk in the city at the end of the eighth episode of *Ulysses*: "Making for the museum gate with long windy steps [Bloom] lifted his eyes. Handsome building. Sir Thomas Deane designed." (Coincidentally, the first edition of *Ulysses* was published in Paris on February 2, 1922, the day Taylor's murder was discovered.)

Intermarriage between the Deane and Tanner families was not unprecedented; Kearns Deane, a brother of Sir Thomas, had married Jane Tanner, daughter of Boyle Tanner, in 1824. Major Kearns Deane-Tanner was apparently the first to conjoin the family names with a hyphen, which his brother Dr. Charlie did not use. The *Boston Globe* reported that Major Deane-Tanner acted as the agent in Ireland for the Duke of Devonshire's landed estates in Waterford, Cork, and southern Ireland. The same source also revealed that the major "kept a stud of fast horses."

What stories of the childhood and youth of William Desmond Taylor (as we'll continue to call him) can be believed? Edward J. Bruen of Chicago said he "knew the Tanner boys in Ireland" and described Major Tanner as having "a violent temper, which led to squabbles with the boy, who ran away at fifteen and entered a military college in England. He left college and went to Canada where he joined the Northwest Mounted Police." But there is no record of Taylor's going to college or having served with the Royal Canadian Mounties.

In a 1914 studio biography, written or vetted by Taylor, he claimed he "was educated at Clifton College, England, where he excelled in hurdles and rowing. His ambition was to go into the army and he was duly examined but failed the eyesight test and had to abandon the idea. Instead he went to France and Germany to study languages [engineering, in another version] and finally came to America and ranched in southwest Kansas." Taylor never attended Clifton College, the English public school near Bristol, according to the headmaster; it was his younger brother Denis who was enrolled there in the preparatory school, Poole's House. Though Taylor was a well-bred, polished, and highly literate man, conversant with French and German, the only college he seems to have attended was that of hard knocks. Yet he was clearly well educated, perhaps by tutors in his youth. He also made himself an autodidact through omnivorous reading.

The single believable fact concerning his youth is that he got into trouble with his father over something, as young men in their teens often do, and left home. But bad eyesight? If Taylor's ambition, as he said, was to enlist, even a hot-tempered father would have had to acknowledge that bad eyes are not the son's fault. And Taylor *did* have eye trouble; he wore glasses at work on movie sets, though not usually in photos, and in 1920 his doctor ordered him to rest his "kleig eyes" for several weeks. No, it sounds as if the rift occurred over something considered much more serious in that Victorian era, such as woman trouble. When Taylor worked at the Balboa film company in 1914, he confessed to his producer that he had spent three years in prison to "protect the honor of a woman he loved." This happens to be the plot of a Balboa film, *The Judge's Wife*, in which Taylor directed Neva Gerber, an actress who was then his fiancée (they never married). The fact that real-life stories can be dramatized as readily as invented stories makes it no easier to know which is which—just as in many aspects of this murder case, there is often no way to distinguish reality from fantasy.

A melodramatic incident of Taylor's youth was revealed by "an old family coachman and caretaker of the estate at Cappoquin," William Coss, who called the lad "the most generous and openhearted young man imaginable." This putative family retainer told a Hearst reporter that Major Tanner went into "a wild Irish rage" and banished his son from the house and forbade him even to speak to other family members—because he failed the eye test. "The lad's position was pitiful. He was forced to wear rags and tatters a beggar would scorn." Irish hyperbole, of course, but old Coss, if he was not invented by the reporter, enjoyed piling on the details: "We servants on the estate pitied the poor unfortunate lad, and when we got the opportunity smuggled food to him. When old Major Tanner was away, we helped William construct an outhouse in a far corner of the great estate where he lived by himself." The reporter then visited the grounds with Coss and made a slight alteration in the legend: "We made our way to a far corner where still stands the small doghouse-like shack which Taylor built alone with his own bare hands, and in which he lived for months." Oddly, Coss placed Taylor's birth in 1877, an incorrect date given in all the newspapers; one would expect an old family retainer not to be five years off regarding the birthday of the eldest son.

Whatever William had done that offended his father—if not a crime, could it have been the explosive subject of politics, the young man siding with Uncle Charlie?—he decided to make a break and leave home. Thus Taylor turned into a wanderer and an actor, who adopted new identities from that point onward. Using his second and third names, Cunningham Deane, he decided to go on the stage in England. It was 1890, and he was eighteen.

He started on the road in Manchester, where the actor-manager Sir Charles Hawtrey, starring in a revival of his own play, *The Private Secretary*, gave the newcomer his first small part. Hawtrey (1855–1923), the son of an Eton headmaster, had adapted this German play by Von Moser to an English setting and made a fortune by producing it himself. It had its premiere in London in 1882, when Taylor was ten, and became a long-standing hit. (Somerset Maugham, in his preface to Hawtrey's autobiography, said the actor was much more interested in horse racing than in the theater: "He could not remember the titles of half the plays he acted in, but he never forgot the name of a horse.") Unsurprisingly, though Hawtrey outlived Taylor, whose murder was international news, he failed to mention him in his book.

When the revival of *The Private Secretary* reached London in 1890, with the new young actor cast in a minor role, friends of the Deane-Tanners saw him. In a fury, his father informed William that no son of Major Deane-Tanner could appear on the stage—not in England, at any rate. The major enrolled his son in a colony called Runnymede, established in America by another Anglo-Irishman, Ned Turnley. There the black-sheep sons of good families were to be turned into gentleman farmers. Young William, not quite nineteen, found himself exiled to Kansas.

Apparently he stuck it out at Runnymede for eighteen months. The only aspect of the place that interested him was horses—their breeding, training, and racing. He had grown up with his father's horses in Ireland, and his one outstanding gift as a movie actor was to be his fine horsemanship. But the breeding of racehorses is filled with pitfalls, and the Runnymede project was a financial failure. Taylor, unwilling to return home, stayed on in America and struck out on his own. Though he kept in touch with his mother and sisters, Taylor found that his

55

allowance had been cut. He was in for hard times.

Details of his years as a common laborer, waiter, railroad hand, gambler, and adventurer—before his return to the stage in 1894–95—would slowly emerge years later in the press. A California businessman, who refused to give his name to the *Los Angeles Record*, revealed that thirty years earlier, in the winter of 1892, he had met Taylor in Kansas City, Missouri.

"Taylor or Tanner had been working as a railroad yardman in Kansas City," he said. "We both became canvassers for magazine subscriptions, working Leavenworth and Atchison in Kansas and St. Joseph in Missouri." On one occasion, Taylor "revealed many facts concerning his early life." They had met Joseph McInerny, proprietor of the Savoy Hotel in St. Joseph, and Taylor told them he was "the second son of a Major Tanner [he was, of course, the eldest son] and had an uncle, a Dr. Tanner, who was a member of Parliament. He had come to America in 1890 and lived with a number of 'remittance men' near Harper, Kansas, where a racehorse venture failed."

His family sent their son a check every three months, and, said the friend,

> we would dine well for two or three days after that. During the winters of our association, we nursed each other through serious illnesses. I next met Tanner in the winter of 1893 in Chicago. He had just come from St. Paul where, with another man, he had been running a ten-and-fifteen-cent restaurant. We were both pretty well broke. We got a job canvassing in country towns. Once, with a four-dollar advance, we went into a basement gambling-room and shot

craps until we had several hundred dollars. We re-
deemed our overcoats from the pawnshop and had a
big feed. I remember the fun we had talking French
and German to the waiter. Tanner had been educated
at Eaton [*sic*] or Woolwich. He was a good mixer,
but quiet. When I knew him, he carried a picture
of a girl with whom he had been in love in England.
He railed against his family a good deal.

The unnamed narrator said he had gone to the Los
Angeles mortuary to see the body; he was certain that
William Desmond Taylor was the man he had known as
Tanner. The restaurant man for whom Taylor had worked
in St. Paul, named L. A. Wiley, came forward to add
another small piece to the mosaic of the young man's life
at age twenty-one:

Tanner came to my restaurant in 1893 without a
nickel, and volunteered to work for his room and
board. He was an unusually well educated fellow.
He spoke several languages and entertained with
many stories and poems. But underneath his good
nature there was something mysterious. He always
seemed worried. This was during the time of the
Chicago World's Fair. Tanner didn't stay as a waiter
much more than three months. I went to Chicago with
him and I last saw him on State Street. He said,
"Goodby, Wiley, I'll never forget you and I hope we
meet again."

A photo of the St. Paul staff, which included two women,
was taken in front of the restaurant and showed Wiley
and a mustached Taylor standing outside in long white
aprons.

A younger Taylor in white tie, the "gentleman actor."

It was around 1895 that Taylor decided to resume the name Cunningham Deane and return to the stage. He said he joined Fanny Davenport's company in New York for the last three years of her life. Fanny was the daughter of the famous actor Edward Loomis Davenport of Boston, whose Hamlet was rated second only to Edwin Booth's in America. In the 1880s, Fanny formed her own company after acquiring exclusive American stage rights to Sardou's *La Tosca, Fédora, Cléopatra,* and *Gismonda,* all surefire hits and in all of which Deane was to play minor roles.

According to the *Boston Globe,* Cunningham Deane made theatrical news in that city by substituting at the Castle Square Theater one night, "at a few hours' notice," for an actor who was taken ill. The critic wrote: "Under the circumstances, Mr. Deane was very satisfactory in the part of a bank cashier and deserves thanks for saving the performance."

Cunningham Deane had the small part of Count Dunois when Fanny Davenport opened in Boston late in 1897 with a new play about Joan of Arc, by Frances Aymar Mathews. (The *Transcript* critic clobbered the play as a distortion of history; when Charles VII attempts to rape her, Joan cries out: "Not that, Sire, not that!") By the time it opened in New York the following month, Deane had been promoted to the more important role of Guy de Laval, and a reviewer said: "Cunningham Deane was a manly and effective young officer, de Laval."

In his monumental *Annals of the New York Stage,* George Odell is unflattering about Fanny's Cleopatra: "She had been a plump and pleasing young woman in her prime in Augustin Daly's company, but her Cleopatra was neither young, nor serpentine, nor lithe; it was rather

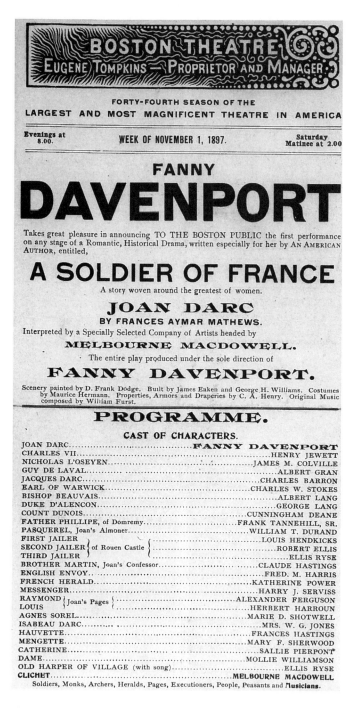

FANNY
DAVENPORT

Takes great pleasure in announcing TO THE BOSTON PUBLIC the first performance on any stage of a Romantic, Historical Drama, written especially for her by AN AMERICAN AUTHOR, entitled,

A SOLDIER OF FRANCE

A story woven around the greatest of women.

JOAN DARC
BY FRANCES AYMAR MATHEWS.

Interpreted by a Specially Selected Company of Artists headed by

MELBOURNE MACDOWELL.

· The entire play produced under the sole direction of

FANNY DAVENPORT.

Scenery painted by D. Frank Dodge. Built by James Eaken and George H. Williams. Costumes by Maurice Hermann. Properties, Armors and Draperies by C. A. Henry. Original Music composed by William Furst.

PROGRAMME.

CAST OF CHARACTERS.

JOAN DARC	FANNY DAVENPORT
CHARLES VII	HENRY JEWETT
NICHOLAS L'OSEYEN	JAMES M. COLVILLE
GUY DE LAVAL	ALBERT GRAN
JACQUES DARC	CHARLES BARRON
EARL OF WARWICK	CHARLES W. STOKES
BISHOP BEAUVAIS	ALBERT LANG
DUKE D'ALENCON	GEORGE LANG
COUNT DUNOIS	CUNNINGHAM DEANE
FATHER PHILLIPE, of Domremy	FRANK TANNEHILL, SR.
PASQUEREL, Joan's Almoner	WILLIAM T. DURAND
FIRST JAILER SECOND JAILER of Rouen Castle THIRD JAILER	LOUIS HENDKICKS ROBERT ELLIS ELLIS RYSE
BROTHER MARTIN, Joan's Confessor	CLAUDE HASTINGS
ENGLISH ENVOY	FRED. M. HARRIS
FRENCH HERALD	KATHERINE POWER
MESSENGER	HARRY J. SERVISS
RAYMOND LOUIS Joan's Pages	ALEXANDER FERGUSON HERBERT HARROUN
AGNES SOREL	MARIE D. SHOTWELL
ISABEAU DARC	MRS. W. G. JONES
HAUVETTE	FRANCES HASTINGS
MENGETTE	MARY F. SHERWOOD
CATHERINE	SALLIE PIERPONT
DAME	MOLLIE WILLIAMSON
OLD HARPER OF VILLAGE (with song)	ELLIS RYSE
CLICHET	MELBOURNE MACDOWELL

Soldiers, Monks, Archers, Heralds, Pages, Executioners, People, Peasants and Musicians.

An 1897 playbill of a Fanny Davenport play,
listing "Cunningham Deane" in cast.

*Fanny Davenport in a studio portrait signed by
Napoleon Sarony of Union Square.*

too adipose." Photos of the actress as Cleopatra confirm that she had a weight problem, and her subsequent illness was attributed to excessive dieting. She died in September 1898, when Taylor was twenty-six. For the time being, his acting career was interrupted.

In May 1899, *Broadway* magazine featured a story about "New York's Prettiest Chorus Girl," Effie Hamilton, who was playing at the American Theater. Effie, twenty-three, was a native of Asbury Park, New Jersey, and her real name was Ethel May Harrison. The photos accompanying the article showed an attractive blonde in various theatrical poses. William C. Deane-Tanner married her at the Little Church Around the Corner on December 7, 1901.

One month after their marriage, Effie opened at the Winter Garden as one of the sextet in a revival of *Floradora*. By the time the show closed in April, after only forty-eight performances, she was pregnant. Ethel May never returned to the theater. On November 15, 1902, the couple's daughter, Ethel Daisy, was born at their town house, 40 Washington Square, New York.

Ethel Daisy's birth certificate listed her father as "Pete" Tanner, his occupation as "Manager, Antique Store." At age thirty, a married man and a father, he had begun a new life. The days of dishing out ten-cent meals, canvassing door to door, working on the railroad, and acting seem to have ended. Taylor was now leading an affluent and thoroughly bourgeois existence, something his temperament would tolerate for seven years only. His sole connection with his past was the membership he retained in the Greenwood Club, a New York actors' organization.

His young wife not only was the daughter of a Wall Street broker but had a wealthy uncle, Henry Jones Braker, the owner of the H. H. Braker pharmaceutical firm. In addition to amassing a fortune from his wholesale drug house, Braker had made millions in real estate. He helped to set up his niece's husband in the antique-furniture business with a loan of $25,000—a vast sum in 1902. Pete Tanner bought into the A. J. Crawford Company, which operated The Little Shop on Murray Hill and the Old English Antique Company at 518 Madison Avenue. Since Ethel May's generous uncle was a childless widower, it seemed certain to everyone, including the newlyweds, that they would be the chief beneficiaries in his will.

Tanner's knowledge of art and antiques, combined with his English accent, good looks, genteel manners, and elegant wardrobe, quickly won the confidence of a wealthy clientele. George Cleveland, an actor friend, acknowledging that Pete was also an interior decorator of skill and ability, said "Many of the handsome residences in New York have been decorated and designed by Taylor." No doubt he incorporated in the décor many pieces of furniture from the Old English Antique Company.

By 1904, the Deane-Tanners had moved from Washington Square to a house in Larchmont, a fashionable suburb in Westchester County, from which he commuted each morning to Grand Central station on the nine-ten train. He became a popular member of the Larchmont Yacht Club, where he served on the arts committee, and he also joined the Dunwoodie Golf Club. One of his colleagues in the antique business, Frank J. Sparrell, said that Tanner was well liked by everyone on the staff, but they noticed he suffered from occasional spells of "terrible feverish neuralgia" and from lapses of memory.

One of his favorite haunts during this period was the bar of the old Imperial Hotel, patronized by a high-living and well-heeled crowd, including Billy Thaw, a yacht club friend. (The most sensational scandal of 1906 was the murder of Stanford White by Billy's half-brother, Harry K. Thaw, whose wife had been another *Floradora* girl, Evelyn Nesbit.) Ethel May Deane-Tanner later admitted she was well aware by 1907 that her husband's attractive looks occasionally involved him with women, but she chose, at least in public, to ignore these infidelities.

That June, to everyone's surprise, Uncle Henry Braker married the rich widow of a banker. Fifteen months later, he fell ill on a voyage to Europe and died in England. Since he had rewritten his will in his wife's favor, the rich Mrs. Braker became even richer. Pete and Ethel May inherited nothing. A clause in Braker's will generously canceled the loan of $25,000 that Pete had never expected to be asked to repay.

It was soon noticed that Tanner was drinking more heavily. There were also rumors that some of the antiques supplied by the A. J. Crawford Company were not authentic. Mrs. William K. Vanderbilt and other members of New York society discovered that among the high-priced objets d'art and furniture they had acquired as genuine antiques were several spurious items. Pete Tanner now seemed to be spending less and less time at the company stores.

In the summer of 1908, a handsome couple registered at a resort hotel in the Adirondacks as Mr. and Mrs. R. P. Townsend, Jr. The man was Pete Tanner, while his unidentified companion was, in the words of the bell captain, "one of the most beautiful women I have ever seen, with blue eyes and masses of golden hair." They stayed to themselves in their cottage on the grounds a whole week and ordered lavish meals sent in, accompanied by the best wines. When Tanner was presented with the bill at the end of their stay, he coolly admitted he had no money. As security, he left his diamond ring with the bookkeeper. (These details surfaced in 1912, when Mrs. Deane-Tanner obtained her divorce on the grounds of adultery. She married again in 1914, when Ethel Daisy was twelve. Her new husband was Edward L. C. Robins, owner of several restaurants, including Delmonico's. This was six years after Pete Tanner's disappearance.)

On September 26, 1908, Taylor, Billy Thaw, and several other friends from the Larchmont Yacht Club watched the Vanderbilt Cup sailing races on Long Island Sound. After the races, Pete holed up in a Manhattan hotel. Before disappearing, he may have met with his younger brother, Denis, who had come to New York after Pete's marriage. Denis had found work in one of the antique shops, where he was praised for his reliability and competence, and he had married. After three days at the hotel, Pete phoned The Little Shop and asked that six hundred dollars in cash be brought to him. The man sent by the shop was surprised to find his boss suffering from a hangover and looking bedraggled enough to be taken for a bum. He said that Taylor, who had shaved off his mustache, was hardly recognizable as the well-groomed vice president they usually saw at the store. Tanner sealed five hundred dollars into an envelope addressed to Ethel May and asked the man to deliver it personally to Mrs. Tanner. The remaining one hundred dollars he put in his pocket. That was the last the antique furniture business saw of Pete Tanner.

After the murder of William Desmond Taylor, Ethel

May Robins—"a woman of charm and courtesy," according to the papers—gave reporters a remarkable interview. She spoke of her former husband without rancor and in terms of admiration. His departure she described as "just like a man picking up his hat to leave the house." Though she knew he had been unfaithful to her, she attributed this and his disappearance to a mental disturbance probably caused by his severe spells of facial neuralgia. She thought he may have also suffered from amnesia. He left behind money and other assets to provide for her and her daughter for a year. Early in their marriage, he had taken her abroad to meet his mother and sister in their new house in Dublin on Fitzwilliam Square. Major Deane-Tanner, his father, had died.

In 1918, Ethel May took her daughter to a movie theater where *Captain Alvarez* was playing and made a discovery. "That's your father," she exclaimed to Ethel Daisy when he appeared on the screen. The girl wrote to him in care of the studio, and thereafter they corresponded regularly. Mrs. Robins later revealed that all three met in New York in 1921, when Taylor was about to sail to Europe. "The exact reason for his leaving," said Mrs. Robins, "has always been a mystery to me." (As he explained it to Neva Gerber, his wife's frequent crying spells made it impossible for him to live with her.) Ethel Daisy said her father told her he had had a lapse of memory for one year after his disappearance from New York in 1908.

Within a month of his departure from New York, Ethel Daisy's father was in fact acting in a stock company just across the river in New Jersey. He had invented a new name and identity, using his initials. He was now

William Desmond Taylor as the star of Captain Alvarez *in 1914.*

The former Mrs. Ethel May Deane-Tanner and daughter Ethel Daisy in 1922.

(and would be to the end) William Desmond Taylor.

Taylor's good friend George Cleveland, a member of the New Jersey stock company, who asked Taylor to be his best man in 1909 when Cleveland married their leading lady, Victory Bateman (the wedding took place in the state of Washington; Cleveland was twenty-two, his wife was thirty-six, Taylor's age), did not let his friendship cloud his critical judgment. "Taylor was a mediocre actor," he said, "but a clever artist. He was exceedingly English in his ways, and a fine fellow."

He said that "Taylor made no attempt I know of to keep the fact that he changed his name a secret. We were going to open an engagement in New Jersey in 1908 and he took the name of William Desmond Taylor. Why, he never said, and we never pried into each other's affairs. . . . Bill was a queer chap when he drank, which was seldom. Usually he devoted all of his attention to the job. Everyone liked him. I certainly never knew such a man as they have described in the papers. Years ago the stock company was stranded in Denver, and Bill obtained a job as a night clerk in a hotel. Once I corresponded with him in Australia."

Inevitably Taylor turned to more dependable ways of making money than acting. He worked as a hotel clerk, factory worker, gold miner, timekeeper, railroad surveyor, among other jobs, for the first four years after adopting his new name. Yet even during the periods of near poverty, he managed to dress in style (when he worked for the Yukon Gold Company for less than six dollars a week, he was known as the "Dude of Dawson City"). He was admired for his horsemanship, his tasteful clothes (including a soft crush hat), his excellence at tennis, and his expertise at cards.

Taylor was always popular with women. When there were big social functions to attend, he wore white tie and tails (an extreme rarity in Dawson City), probably part of the wardrobe that helped him to get theater jobs when the clothes were not in hock. A woman who remembered him as the night clerk at the Interocean Hotel in Cheyenne, Wyoming's largest, said: "He was an outstanding character, quite out of place in such an occupation." Others remembered that when he played in stock in Alaskan towns like Skagway and Fairbanks, he was accompanied by his "sister," an attractive banjo-playing actress with whom he lived.

Publicity—or puffery, as it was then called by theater people—was an art that Taylor mastered. For example, his appearance at the Beck Theater with Victory Bateman was announced, with a streamer headline, in the *Bellingham* (Washington) *Herald* on January 2, 1910, accompanied by a large photo and a text that dealt in superlatives: "One of the handsomest and most talented leading men in the profession, in the person of William Desmond Taylor, begins rehearsals of *Sowing the Wind*. . . . Mr. Taylor is a man of commanding appearance and charming manner, finely educated and of excellent English parentage. He has traveled the world over, and carries with him the air of a man who knows life in all its phases."

A week later, the same newspaper reported: "Taylor Is Mistaken for 'Gentleman Jim' Corbett." The puffery this time was that once, in a San Francisco restaurant, Taylor started to defend his female companion with his fists, but the cad who made an insulting remark fled for his life when some joker shouted, "Watch out, he's Jim Corbett!"

In British Columbia, Taylor worked on the Grand Trunk Railway terminus at Prince Rupert and in a paper mill at Swanson Bay. When he failed as a gold prospector in Colorado, he took a job as a hotel clerk at Telluride. For several months in the Yukon, while working at the Ninety-Below Discovery Mine, he is said to have shared a cabin with Canadian poet Robert W. Service, the author of "The Shooting of Dan McGrew" and other popular ballads, and with "Red" Ashford. The latter, quoting one of Service's lines, described Taylor as sad and sorrowful, "Like a man with a grief you can't control"; he also said Taylor confided that he had had a great love and a great sorrow in his life. It is not difficult to conclude that Taylor regarded himself as a romantic soldier of fortune. A poem he wrote during this period confirms such an image. With echoes of W. E. Henley as well as Robert Service, the poem is chiefly interesting as autobiography:

THE KNOWLEDGE

Man—do you know, have you felt, and seen,
In the wastes of the earth have your footsteps been?
Have you tasted the salt, the deserts trod,
Forsaken all else, forgotten your God?
At the beck and call of a woman's nod,
Have you walked the paths that are mean?

Have you eaten the sweets and spat the gall,
Has your heart beat high at the wanderlust call,
Had rope in hand, or gun in fist,
Been cursed and loved and beaten and missed,
And slept where the wind your brow has kissed?
Have you fought with your back to the wall?

Even so, and from fate you never ran
Though held 'neath narrow society's ban,
Ne'er taken an innocent girl in tow,
Nor lied, nor struck a fallen foe—
Then you have felt *and* seen *and* know
And you'll die as you've lived, a man.

In 1912, Taylor turned up in Hawaii, in the stock company of the Australian producer Harry Corson Clarke, for whom he had also worked "down under." The *Honolulu Advertiser* stated that "Mr. Taylor only recently was induced to return to the stage after spending a winter or two in Alaska. He was in the Boer War and is to some extent a soldier of fortune." The last three words are certainly accurate, but the rest of the sentence is puffery. It was his brother Denis, not he, who fought in the Boer War. There are conflicting accounts of Taylor's movements after he left Clarke's company in March 1912. He may have returned to Alaska, where he was said to have fallen ill. In the fall of that year, Taylor turned up in San Francisco, where a theater friend, Eleanor Gordon, and her husband found him down-and-out and sick again. They supplied him with money and helped him to recuperate. Soon he was on the stage at the Alcazar Theater, whose leading actress was Rhea "Ginger" Mitchell.

The wheel of fortune now turned in Taylor's favor. Thomas Ince, head of the New York Motion Picture Company at Santa Monica, spotted the pair on the stage of the Alcazar and engaged them to act in his films. For William Desmond Taylor, now forty, the worst years of struggle were over.

5

Making It in the Movies

In the light of Taylor's precarious and sometimes wretched existence between 1908 and 1913, his own description of how he broke into the movies (published in the January 1915 issue of *Motion Picture*) reads ironically or, as his forebears might have said, like blarney:

> I entered the pictures as a sort of compromise. I had made several attempts to get away from the stage, and my last venture had been along the lines of mining, when the annoyingly persistent call of the stage came again and, as I did not fancy the small and stuffy dressing-rooms and the continual study, I came to the Coast and deliberately tried to get into the Motion Picture game. There was that about the Kay-Bee camp which appealed, being near the ocean and the delightful scenery, so I applied and got a position with that company and had a taste of the delights of acting in the open.
>
> From now on it's the movies for me, and isn't it

curious that the companies I have worked with have been near the sea? At the Vitagraph, where I played Captain Alvarez in the thrilling photodrama of that name, we were at Santa Monica, and now I am at Long Beach, directing and acting with the Balboa Company. So I can still get my ride, woo nature with her ever-changing scenes, and go in for my swim and enjoy the strong sea air.

The movie fans of 1915 never knew he got his start because Thomas Ince happened to see him on the San Francisco stage. Taylor's first acting job on the screen was in a western, *The Iconoclast* (three reels), filmed at Inceville. According to King Vidor, "Five miles along the California coast north of Santa Monica was a fabulous place called Inceville. It was named after its owner and originator, Thomas Ince. It consisted of a profusion of open stages and false fronts of Western settings so familiar in films of that day. One saw Indian braves biting the dust as their horses were shot out from under them, or United States cavalry racing to the rescue of a besieged wagon train. . . . The topography of Inceville also included the scrub hills of the Santa Monica mountains and the rocky coast line and beaches of the Pacific Ocean."*

Thomas Harper Ince (1882–1924) was an important pioneer moviemaker and an expert self-promoter. His death, after a gastritis attack aboard William Randolph Hearst's yacht, was falsely metamorphosed into a Hollywood murder by poisoning. What put Inceville on the map was the authentic atmosphere the cowboys and Indians of the 101 Ranch Wild West Show contributed to the films, as well as the popularity of the William S. Hart westerns that Ince produced.

* Vidor, *A Tree Is a Tree*, p. 63.

Inceville in 1919, located on the Pacific at Santa Ynez Canyon.

Producer Thomas Ince with a Kay-Bee actor, William Eagleshirt, in 1915.

"The importance of Inceville to the westerns," wrote Kevin Brownlow, "might almost be compared to the importance of Detroit to the automobile." Taylor arrived early in 1913, at a moment when Ince's financial backers included Adam Kessel and Charles Baumann, who backed the Keystone Comedies; their initials made up the Kay-Bee trademark.

Ince's contribution to the silent film is considerable, ranging from *Custer's Last Fight* (1912) to the impressive first version of Eugene O'Neill's *Anna Christie* (1923) with Blanche Sweet and William Russell (which pleased the playwright and obviously influenced the style and costumes of the second version, Garbo's first talkie). His most famous movie was the pacifist tract *Civilization* (1916), released before the United States entered the First World War; it was praised by Woodrow Wilson. To modern eyes, its stagey décor, stiff acting, and at times ludicrous story make it a disappointing film. Early French film critics like Léon Moussinac mistakenly rated Ince "the equal, if not the master, of D. W. Griffith." They correctly praised him for his westerns; for *The Coward* (1915), starring the boyishly charming Charles Ray; and for the realism of many of his films.

Charlie Chaplin gives a nostalgic portrait of Inceville in this era: "Thomas Ince gave barbecues and dances at his studio, which was in the wilds of northern Santa Monica, facing the Pacific Ocean. What wondrous nights —youth and beauty dancing to plaintive music on an open-air stage, with the soft sound of waves pounding on the nearby shore."* The early screenwriter and critic James Shelley Hamilton also experienced an Edenic sense

* Charles Chaplin, *My Autobiography* (New York: Simon & Schuster, 1964), p. 157.

Thomas Ince at Los Angeles depot, departing for New York.

of Hollywood in this period when he visited D. W. Griffith on the set of *Intolerance*. He said that the master had the whole company join hands and snake-dance in a long line around the lot. They were not rehearsing. Rather, "He wanted them all to relax and have fun. You can't imagine how different it was in those days. We all felt that a new era, and a marvelous art, had begun. No cost accounting, no efficiency experts, no ironclad schedules— all that came later."* Chaplin's words reinforce this sense of fellowship and community during the teens in Hollywood: "Each studio was like a family. It was 1914 and I was 25 years old, in the flush of youth and enamored of my work—not alone for the success of it, but for its enchantment."†

All the movies in which Taylor appeared as an actor have disappeared, and apparently it is no great loss. The mannerisms that he and a whole generation of actors inherited from the theater persisted on the early screen. Compare D. W. Griffith's stagey gestures in *Rescued from the Eagle's Nest* (1907) to the naturalism of the actors he directed in *The Musketeers of Pig Alley* (1912). The styles are worlds apart; the camera's liberation from confined rooms and painted sets, its escape into the open air, transformed the aesthetics of the movies.

Taylor's debut in *The Iconoclast* was followed by three two-reelers: *A True Believer*, a Civil War story; *Grand Dad*, and *Retrogression*, all made at Kay-Bee in 1913. He then transferred his acting talents to Vitagraph, one of the oldest New York companies, where Mabel Normand got her start. Vitagraph, following the drift westward, had opened a studio at Santa Monica in 1911 (Warner Bros.

---

* Hamilton in conversation with the author in 1950.
† Ibid.

bought them out in 1925). After ten mediocre films under its aegis, Taylor in 1914 was featured in the six-reel *Captain Alvarez*, with two leading women, Edith Storey and Myrtle Gonzales.

The film presents him as Robert Wainwright, an American who becomes a revolutionary leader in South America under the alias Captain Alvarez. The director was Rollin Sturgeon, a Harvard alumnus who later introduced Taylor to Mabel Normand. Reviewers praised the large-scale battle scenes and Taylor's ride for freedom across a flimsy and dangerously narrow bridge high above a chasm (in the stills, the bridge looks like a single board). Taylor on horseback was in his element. "He has never done anything better than his interpretation of Captain Alvarez," announced *Photoplay*. In the few surviving stills, his acting appears to be stony-faced in the William S. Hart manner. It was when the movie was reissued in 1917 (because by then Edith Storey had become an important star) that Taylor's wife and daughter saw him on the screen for the first time.

William D. Taylor—the usual listing of his name in this period—acted in fifteen movies before he became a director. Aside from his success as Alvarez, his acting had had little impact. Now in his forties, he knew his acting days were numbered. He was fortunate to be able to make the transition from actor to director. According to the director Allan Dwan, an early friend of his, Taylor heard of an opening at the Balboa studio, where they needed someone with previous movie experience. Taylor's mature and self-assured manner got him the job.

At Balboa, he fell in love with Neva Gerber, the heroine of the first film he directed. They became engaged. Neva was a dark-haired society beauty whose father was a well-known criminal lawyer in Chicago and whose grandfather, William Younge, had been governor of Kentucky. Educated at the exclusive Immaculate Heart College in Chicago, she was living with her mother and little daughter in Hollywood; she had left her husband, an older man, and was awaiting a divorce. *The Awakening*, the three-reeler that marked Taylor's directorial debut, was released in October 1914. Neva also appeared in Taylor's next four Balboa films.

The Balboa Amusement Production Company, which in 1913 had taken over the abandoned Edison studios at Long Beach, was run by the Horkheimer brothers, whose finances were shaky. Almost anything seems to have been possible in those days: Terry Ramsaye relates that when the sheriff and his deputies arrived one day to seize the studio for unpaid debts, the Horkheimers conned them into acting as a sheriff's posse in front of the cameras, not only delaying their mission but guaranteeing the release of the film, since the lawmen wanted their friends to see them in the movies. Balboa, which lasted only a few years, ceased production in 1917. It was H. H. Horkheimer to whom Taylor confessed an episode from his past that may or may not have been true—his three years in prison to "protect the honor of a woman he loved." *The Judge's Wife*, its script reflecting this theme, was released in November 1914, with Neva Gerber in the lead.

Neva is one of the few sources of information about the private life of William Desmond Taylor. Their love affair lasted five years, during which they could not marry because Neva's husband resisted the divorce. Taylor had of course told her about his wife and child, and he was free to marry again since Ethel May had won a divorce.

Actress Neva Gerber in 1917–18.

He also told Neva he had left his wife because of her frequent crying spells. He said he could not bear to see a woman cry.

Like all the women close to Taylor, Neva praised him highly: "He was the soul of honor, a man of personal culture, education and refinement. I have never known a finer or better man." She was impressed by his generosity: "It is true that Mr. Taylor gave me three cars—first, an old one that he had used and later two new ones he purchased in my name. When he began giving me presents of autos and jewelry—and yes, money—we were engaged. We expected to be married as soon as I got my divorce and they [the presents] did not seem anything out of the way to either of us."

He was so determined to make good as a director, she said, that after completing a picture he would be in a state of total nervous exhaustion: "At such times he would sink to such depths of despair that his whole body seemed racked as if in physical torture." These black moods of his frightened her. The attacks seemed to resemble the spells of neuralgia he had exhibited at the antique store. When he was in this state, Neva said, "He would walk the floor and wring his hands, asking, 'Why do I have to keep up this battle? Is it worthwhile to continue this struggle of existence? With all the odds against me, is the struggle really worth it?' " The implied threat of suicide in these words worried her. When she asked, "What do you mean?" he replied, "Oh, my health is so bad! I have no stomach left, I can't eat anything." Since he appeared so athletic—he swam almost every day and usually looked trim and fit—she was puzzled. Yet he blamed his recurrent fits of depression on his "bad health" and "nerves." As he lived alone, she wondered if his unhappy moods

William Desmond Taylor in 1917.

were brought on by loneliness. She urged him to live at a hotel or a men's club, but he replied that he needed solitude for his creative work.

After finishing a movie, he often took a trip into the wilderness in northern California, in order, he said, "to commune with nature and recuperate." She thought he went on these trips alone, but he once inadvertently mentioned a traveling companion, and when she questioned this, he said, "Oh, he was just a hitchhiker I met by chance." It may have been his brother Denis, of whose existence Neva was unaware.

If William Desmond Taylor's life could be considered mysterious, that of his younger brother Denis was doubly so. He not only seemed to live in his brother's shadow, but copied his behavior as consistently as if he *were* his brother's shadow. Denis Gage Deane-Tanner was four years junior to his brother and the last of his parents' four children. After he left Poole's House at Clifton College at age thirteen in December 1889, nothing is on record until the Boer War (1899–1902), when, with his father's encouragement and blessing, he served as a lieutenant in the British Army in South Africa. He came to New York in 1903, after William's marriage, and worked in the antique furniture business. In 1907, he married Ada Brennan; they had three children, one of whom died in infancy. In 1908, after William abandoned his family, Denis became the manager of an antique store and was well regarded by his employer. It was not until 1912, at a time when his wife was being treated for tuberculosis in the Adirondacks, that he followed his brother's example and deserted his family. Ada never saw her husband again, though she conducted a long search, with the help of an insurance company that had issued a policy on his life.

Taylor's younger brother Denis Deane-Tanner.

Denis may have joined William in the Yukon before he surfaced in the minor role of a blacksmith in *Captain Alvarez*.

Ada, having moved to Monrovia, California, with her daughters after seeing him on the screen, could not locate her husband in Hollywood, but she succeeded in tracking down and confronting her brother-in-law in his Paramount office. Taylor stonily denied he was Deane-Tanner, until Ada broke down crying and said she was in desperate financial need. He then put her on a monthly allowance of fifty dollars; one of the last checks he signed was made out to Ada as of February 1, 1922. Art director George Hopkins confirmed the fact that Denis worked surreptitiously for his brother at Paramount; apparently he turned up at odd hours during the night and early morning. After Taylor's murder, no trace of Denis Deane-Tanner was ever found.

Neva Gerber knew nothing of Denis, but she came to know William intimately enough to describe the man behind the mask: "He frequently referred in a vague way to great sorrows he had had, and of not making the most he might have out of his life. I would try to cheer him up, by telling him what a wonderful director he had become in such a short time, and that he had great fame and success ahead of him. Sometimes he would throw off his despairing mood, but it began to return more and more frequently. I do not think the general public knew anything about his despondent side, as he was a very silent and self-contained man."

Neva and Taylor called off their engagement early in 1919. It was done by mutual consent and without ill will. She admitted that she and her mother felt it would be unwise for her to risk an uncertain second marriage. Taylor, she said, had returned from military service in Europe more despondent than ever, even though he was at the height of his career and was now the president of the Motion Picture Directors Association. He told her with great bitterness that he had learned in England that his mother had been killed in a German air raid and that his sister's husband, an officer in the British Army, had been killed in action. Oddly, he also told Neva that his daughter had been killed in London. Was he lying about Ethel Daisy to evoke sympathy, or was there an earlier, illegitimate daughter, born abroad? It is impossible to know.

Taylor and Neva remained friends after their breakup and kept in touch. She had tried to open a boutique with his financial help. Shortly before his murder, Taylor sent her a gift of five hundred dollars when, she said, her "business affairs were in pretty much of a jam."

After Balboa, Taylor's next job established him as a director with a future, at a moment when the movie business was benefiting from the sensational success of *The Birth of a Nation*. Allan Dwan hired Taylor at the American Film Company—popularly known as the Flying "A"—a leading firm whose studios and laboratories at Santa Barbara were among the most technically advanced anywhere. The long-lived Dwan (1885–1981), whose most famous film among the hundreds he directed over a long career was *Robin Hood* (1922), sized Taylor up as a reliable professional. (Dwan also gave a start to the young King Vidor and to Victor Fleming, whose peak was reached with *Gone With the Wind*.) Soon after Taylor started at American, he was handed a tough assignment.

Flying "A" had just launched its most ambitious project, a highly publicized and lengthy serial of sixty reels —thirty episodes of two reels each—entitled *The Diamond From the Sky*. The script, which had won a ten-thousand-dollar prize contest conducted by the *Chicago Tribune*, was written by a newspaperman, Roy L. McCardell. After the serial was completed, it was promoted with inflated advertising that called it "emphatically the greatest film ever produced, a ceaseless cataract of action, the Serial Wonderful."

Flying "A" wanted Mary Pickford for the leading role and offered her four thousand dollars a week. She refused, suggesting that they could use the Pickford name by hiring her sister Lottie. They signed up Lottie, unaware that she drank too much and had just become pregnant. Jacques Jaccard, a former cameraman, had started off as the director and had put ten episodes, or one-third of the serial, in the can when he hit a snag. He turned for advice to the new director on the lot, William Desmond Taylor, who confidently showed Jaccard how to do the scenes. At this point, Jaccard received a better offer from Universal, which he accepted. Taylor's chance had come: Flying "A" needed his help to bring off the remaining episodes, and he was put in charge.

The Diamond From the Sky was later published as a

OPPOSITE: *William Desmond Taylor with the cast he directed in the serial* The Diamond From the Sky. *He is at center, with folded arms; Lottie Pickford at piano, far right, with Irving Cummings; William Russell seated at far left, next to Charlotte Burton.*

440-page book,* illustrated with sixteen stills from the movie. As one would expect of a cliff-hanging serial, it is a gothic tale of gypsies, a mix-up of babies, conflicting claims to an earldom, and an endless search for the heirloom—a great diamond, which had fallen to the earth in a meteor centuries earlier. The diamond keeps getting into the wrong hands, like those of the archvillainess who controls the hero with morphine: "We will have him lie down, sit up, roll over and play dead, just as we say. Talk of black magic, it's nothing to white magic—morphine sulfate."

In one interview, Taylor referred to *The Diamond From the Sky* as "an education." He approached it "as an experimental laboratory, to try out effects. We had people falling from balloons, autos going over cliffs, and used all kinds of trained animals, from an elephant to an octopus." Several of the serial's more sinister episodes involved the hero in the toils of dope—morphine. Allan Dwan told King Vidor that Taylor had a personal crusade against dope as early as 1915: "I do know that Taylor had a thing about the use of dope, and was very much against its use on the set. He actively tried to stop the drifters who used to come up from Los Angeles with cocaine and opium. There were as many dope dealers as there were prostitutes and, believe me, there was never a shortage of prostitutes. Taylor was known to throw a mean lecture on the evils of drugs to his company of actors."

Dwan also defended Taylor's character, which news reports had blackened: "The reporters got him wrong. Taylor was a gentleman and an artist. He was fair,

* Roy L. McCardell, *The Diamond From the Sky: A Romantic Novel* (New York: G. W. Dillingham, 1916).

friendly, and extremely talented—not at all the libertine the newspaper stories painted after his death."

Taylor completed *The Diamond From the Sky* on schedule. The progress of Lottie Pickford's pregnancy during the seven months she starred in the film was one of his biggest headaches. In the later episodes, Taylor used a double in the long shots, and in medium shots showed Lottie half hidden or otherwise camouflaged behind various props. The group photo taken on the completion of the serial shows William Desmond Taylor in the center, dominating the cast with folded arms, a stern but not unpleasant look on his long, aristocratic face, while Lottie sits before a piano at the right, her back one-third to the camera; she wears a long velvet cloak and a fur piece, which almost but not quite conceal her interesting condition. The great box-office success of *The Diamond From the Sky* more than justified the two-carat diamond ring that Flying "A" presented to Taylor in gratitude; it was on his finger when his murdered body was found.

In the far left of the group photo, wearing flashy clothes, a high stiff collar, and two-tone shoes, sits young William Russell, who had a big part in the serial and who later played opposite Blanche Sweet in *Anna Christie* (1923). The six-foot-two, two-hundred-six-pound Russell, who had known Taylor as Deane-Tanner in New York, rushed to his defense when the post-murder smear of the director's character was at its height. He said they had met in 1908 at the Greenwood Club, where "a certain dignity and courtliness" in Taylor's manner had so impressed the younger man that "I remembered him instantly" when they met on the set. Taylor told him he had changed his name for professional reasons. Russell saw nothing significant in this, since changed names were commonplace among actors. Like Neva Gerber, Russell was aware of Taylor's fits of depression and his air of loneliness.

> Taylor seemed depressed when I met him here. Liking and admiring him as I did, I worried about him and induced him to come and live with me, and for nearly a year we maintained bachelor quarters together on Flower Street. He often spoke to me of his little girl [Ethel Daisy was twelve in 1915], and always with the greatest affection, and several times he mentioned having a brother in New York. I never heard him speak slightingly or disrespectfully of a woman, and never knew him to do a dishonorable or unkind act. As one of his closest friends, I personally resent any insinuation that might be made against his character. . . .

Russell's tribute to his dead friend went further:

> If women were infatuated with him, it was only natural. His manner, his very aloofness, attracted them, and if they wrote him wild love notes [a reference to Mary Miles Minter], was he to blame? If he gave women money, it was because in the generosity of his big heart he wanted to help them, wanted to keep them from the necessity of asking other men for it. If Taylor sometimes associated with people who were not altogether what they should be morally, it was because he had faith that in every human being there is a spark of divinity. He not only tried but often succeeded in assisting many to rise above the lesser things of earth.

Another friend of Taylor's was Winifred Kingston, whom he had directed in *Davy Crockett* (1916), in which her husband, Dustin Farnum, starred. She spoke of their friendship in an interview after the murder:

> It so happened that both Mr. Taylor and I were English. That is, he was Irish but a British subject and educated as an Englishman and with the British Army traditions of his family behind him. We Britishers are naturally reserved and don't usually tell intimate things to others. But early in the history of film Mr. Taylor and I became acquainted, back in the Balboa days. As I was English, we became somewhat more friendly than most. For example, he told me about having been married and having a child, and also about having been divorced. I never thought anything in particular about it and don't see why anyone is surprised to learn about that.
>
> It's not unusual either that he should have had my photograph on his desk. He directed me in any number of pictures and for years we had been good friends. I never knew he changed his name on coming out here, but that fact doesn't seem to be important. I don't see where any of this old history helps to solve the mystery of his death.
>
> I think everything points to this man, Sands. While [playwright] Edward Knoblock was living as a guest at Mr. Taylor's home, Sands went downtown and bought lingerie which I understand he gave to a girl he was interested in. All of this he charged to Mr. Taylor's account. Sands also presented Mr. Knoblock with a bill amounting to some hundreds of dol-

lars for groceries while he was a guest at the house. Mr. Knoblock, being a gentleman, paid the bill and when Mr. Taylor returned he was naturally outraged. Mr. Taylor also told me about the document [written by Sands on parchment], and laughed about it. This led me to believe that the man was mentally deranged. He is the only one I can think of who might have killed Mr. Taylor.

The testimony of producer Jesse Lasky, Taylor's employer, is also an essential part of his portrait as sketched by the people closest to him: "He was a handsome Englishman of such quiet dignity and quality that we used him as Exhibit A when we wanted to show off Hollywood's culture and refinement. . . . We usually managed to score a point for Hollywood's prestige by inviting William Desmond Taylor and seating him next to a society leader. He invariably made a favorable impression."*

Although there was a period during which Mary Miles Minter and Taylor both worked at American/Flying "A," oddly enough they never met. Mary made twenty-four films there, shepherded by her ambitious mother, but it was not until her move to Paramount that she first met Taylor.

Before Taylor's enlistment in the Canadian Army in the summer of 1918, director Rollin Sturgeon had introduced him to the other star in the murder case, Mabel Normand. They both had apartments in the Baltic, at 1127 Orange in Hollywood, Mabel on the second floor and Taylor on the fourth. This was the period when Mabel left Keystone and signed as a major star in Sam Goldwyn's

* Lasky, *I Blow My Own Horn*, p. 154.

new company. After Taylor's engagement to Neva Gerber was broken in 1919, he and Mabel became intimate friends. Early in their friendship, as U.S. Attorney Tom Green, stationed in Los Angeles, was soon to reveal, Mabel "confessed her [drug] habit" to Taylor and "asked him to do everything possible to save her." In many ways, Mabel's story is the most tragic of those involved in the case.

6

The Woman in Blue

Aftter the success of *The Diamond From the Sky*, William Desmond Taylor was ready for the most important step in his career. He moved to Pallas Pictures, which soon merged into Paramount. The woman responsible for hiring him wielded the greatest influence in his professional life.

Julia Crawford Ivers (1867–1930) was an anomaly in Hollywood. While everyone else sought publicity by every means, she never granted an interview to any trade or fan magazine, never advertised in the directories; no photograph of her has been found. She has been called a mystery woman because so little is known about her. Yet she had scores of films to her credit, not only as a scriptwriter, but as a director and producer. Other early women careerists in the movies, like Frances Marion, Lois Weber, Ida May Park, Dorothy Arzner, Jeanie MacPherson, Margery Wilson, and Alice Guy-Blaché, have all been written about or wrote books of their own, yet in

*Early Women Directors,** Anthony Slide admits that less is known about Julia Crawford Ivers than about any of her contemporaries.

Ivers is called "the second woman to have directed a motion picture," following in the footsteps of the pioneer, Madame Guy-Blaché at Pathé. Ivers not only directed Lenore Ulric's early movie *The Heart of Paula*, in April 1916 at Pallas, but also wrote the script. The film's outdoor photography in Mexico, singled out for praise by the reviewers, was the camera work of her son.

Julia Ivers's grandson, James Van Trees, Jr., has revealed that she was born in Los Angeles on October 3, 1867. Her father, Dr. James Crawford, was a dental surgeon who in his youth had been a friend of Mark Twain, with whom he traveled through the California mining camps. While in her twenties, Julia married Frank Van Trees and their son became a master cameraman and one of the founders and a president of the American Society of Cinematographers. (James Crawford Van Trees, A.S.C., who accompanied his mother to Taylor's house on the morning the murder was discovered, died at age eighty-three in 1973.) Divorcing Frank Van Trees, she married Oliver Ivers.

Ivers was the partner of Frank C. Garbutt, a Los Angeles entrepreneur who made a fortune in real estate, oil, and banking. Garbutt entered the movie business by financing Hobart Bosworth, a pioneer filmmaker and one of the first actors to surface in Hollywood. The Garbutt-Bosworth alliance formed two companies, Pallas Pictures and (with the Broadway producer Oliver Morosco) Morosco Pictures. In 1914, both companies signed an agree-

* Anthony Slide, *Early Women Directors* (New York: A. S. Barnes; London: Thomas Yoseloff, 1977), p. 110.

ment to join with the former Jesse Lasky Feature Play Company (in which Lasky, his brother-in-law Sam Goldwyn, and Cecil DeMille had been associated) and with Adolph Zukor's Famous Players. That is how Paramount was born. Charles Eyton, Julia Ivers's and Frank Garbutt's longtime associate at Morosco-Bosworth, became general manager of the major new studio.

Julia Ivers's film career started under Frank Garbutt after Oliver Ivers's death. According to her grandson, "Mr. Garbutt invited my grandmother to a private showing of a film he was almost ready to release," and Ivers's suggestions for improving it so impressed him that "from there on she was on his payroll." She had done some writing of her own and had taken several writing courses at California colleges. In addition to serving as scenario editor at the modern Morosco-Bosworth studios, which Garbutt opened on Occidental Boulevard in Close Range, a Los Angeles suburb, Ivers directed several films and supervised others, while also writing scripts for the company.

It was Grover Jones, an art director, designer, and dresser of sets at Paramount, who first called her "the woman in blue," in his memoirs. William Desmond Taylor had come to Pallas-Paramount shortly after Grover Jones did, "bringing with him a most up-to-date wardrobe, and a set of manners that were almost too perfect," Jones wrote.* In those days, some of the studio's stages were still exposed to the open air. When there was rain or a heavy fog, Jones said, he had to "rush to these sets and cover the furniture," often working after hours. "I was always certain to meet Taylor," he explained, be-

* Grover Jones, "Magic Lantern." Part III of the serialization in the *Saturday Evening Post*, January 23, 1937, pp. 16–17, 44–49.

cause the director usually stayed late "for the purpose of discussing with the script-writer the detailed routine" of the action he planned to shoot the following day.

"Always," said Jones, "his companion was a little woman dressed in blue. She never spoke to me, but I noticed that Taylor paid the strictest attention to everything she said." Sometimes she would completely change a routine, which meant that Jones had to re-dress the set. After Taylor's murder, Jones watched the newspapers carefully to see if a photograph of the woman in blue would turn up; it never did. (Four years after Taylor's death, Jones and his wife were on location, when "a limousine rolled up and a liveried chauffeur opened the door. The woman in blue stepped out."* That was in 1926, when Julia Ivers was still writing scripts for Paramount. He never saw her again.) The last film Ivers directed was *The White Flower*, filmed in Hawaii with Betty Compson and Edmund Lowe. Ivers wrote and produced it, and according to James Van Trees, Jr., "My father photographed the picture in Hawaii, where they set up a lab and developed the negative." Paramount arranged its premiere at the Rialto in New York on April 25, 1923; Ivers died seven years later.

Taylor's office at Paramount was next door to Julia Ivers'. Every noon she prepared a simple lunch for him, following a special diet to alleviate his attacks of indigestion, presumably from a stomach ulcer. It was Taylor's custom to serve tea on the set in the late afternoon, and Mrs. Ivers always poured. After the murder, reporters readily concluded that she was in love with him. According to the *Chicago American*: "Mrs. Ivers, the woman who really loved William Desmond Taylor, knew the secrets

* "Magic Lantern," p. 49.

under the mask he turned to the world. For years she had been laboring by his side, uncomplaining and unselfish, even when he was carrying on affairs with other women. She advised him and took care of him. Since the tragedy, she has not been seen in filmland. In the seclusion of her home and in the deepest mourning, she has grieved over the eternal parting with her great love."

Since she attended the inquest, prepared to testify, it seems bizarre that she was not asked to do so. The final indignity, the allegation that *she* might have committed the murder, surfaced in the *Baltimore American*: "This is a confidential theory the police are investigating. Mrs. Julia Crawford Ivers, who wrote several of his scenarios, is about his own age [she was five years older]. Rumors are that she was infatuated with him and insanely jealous of his attentions to the queens of the movie world. The bullet which killed Taylor was a .38 calibre, soft nose [it was hard-nosed] of old design. The old-style bullet supports the theory that the weapon may have been long in her family." The rumored investigation led nowhere. The concept of the family gun was baseless.

It is incredible that neither the police nor the press circulated a description of the stranger Faith MacLean saw leaving Taylor's house after the murder. The sheriff's "theory" that the killer "may have been" a woman provided reporters with reams of speculative copy far removed from the only solid evidence the police had. (Neither Mrs. Ivers, whom Grover Jones described as a little woman, nor Charlotte Shelby—Mary Miles Minter's mother—fits the MacLean description.)

Averse as Mrs. Ivers was to the press and publicity, her tongue seems to have been loosened by the shock of

Taylor's murder. On the day of his funeral, she released this statement:

> Today the friends of William D. Taylor, and they are legion, will gather to pay the last tribute to the man they love. . . . I have worked side by side with him for seven years. We have solved many difficult problems together, sometimes pleasant, sometimes unpleasant—always hard, trying, nerve-wracking. And during all those years of close association I have never known him to do one unkind, ungenerous act. I have known hundreds of instances of open-handed generosity. . . .
>
> This man was shot in the back by a cowardly assassin. He was given no opportunity to defend himself, for he did not know the meaning of the word fear. And more cowardly than the assassin's bullet is the tongue of scandal which is striking at his reputation. His friends know that, when it is all over, the character of Mr. Taylor will stand, as it always has stood, for everything that is fine and worthwhile.

The *Los Angeles Examiner* reported Mrs. Ivers's description of Taylor as a man "who needed a sister's companionship and understanding." When he turned to her for help, it was "as a confiding big brother." She said, "One couldn't be in the presence of Mr. Taylor for five minutes without instinctively realizing one was facing a man of keen intellect, sympathetic understanding, and unbounded kindliness—a truly great man." She cited what she said was his favorite motto: *"The only things we really keep are the things we give away."* When she was asked what the private man was like, she replied:

"I know of no words that can fully describe my feeling toward Mr. Taylor. Without reservation I can say that, of all those with whom I have ever been associated, he was a man of the highest ideals.... His keen and sparkling mind, far-reaching vision, and love of things noble and exemplary placed him on a pedestal."

She told several stories of his unusual generosity. A young director stranded in Honolulu, for example, appealed to Taylor for help.

At once a cable for five thousand dollars was on its way. Mr. Taylor had no expectation of ever seeing the money again. . . . A short time ago an extra girl lost her purse in the studio; he heard of her plight and started a collection with a substantial contribution of his own. Many of the veterans made cripples in the late war were on his payroll for financial help. A few weeks before this great tragedy, he was the first one to be approached for a benefit and gave a check for $500 immediately.

As I stood outside his door, after I heard of the terrible tragedy, my thought was this: "Whatever resources he might have in the bank, he has earned something rarer—the love and gratitude of hundreds." And he understood human nature. Sometimes players came on the set with such inexpressive countenances it seemed as if only a wizard could make actors out of them. But he drew them out, as the camera clicked. He had an almost uncanny understanding of subtle things, which only someone with the soul of an artist could conceive.

Apparently she knew all about his prospecting years in the Yukon: "This man, who stood for everything that was fine and clean in pictures, is known to have declared that, if it were necessary to his success to produce unclean pictures, he would go back to the white clean snows of Alaska and dig his living again out of the ground."

The seven years from 1915 until his death constitute the most successful and productive period of Taylor's career. He directed forty films for Paramount, with actresses like Mary Pickford, Constance Talmadge, Mary Miles Minter, Betty Compson, Agnes Ayres, May McAvoy, Elsie Janis, Ethel Clayton, Kathlyn Williams, Louise Huff, Elsie Ferguson, Winifred Kingston, Lila Lee, and ZaSu Pitts; and such actors as Wallace Reid, Jack Pickford, Dustin Farnum, Milton Sills, Wallace Beery, Theodore Roberts, Norman Kerry, Monte Blue, George Beban, Douglas MacLean, Paul Kelly, Theodore Kosloff, Edmund Lowe, Jack Hoxie, House Peters, and Conrad Nagel. The following list includes all the films he directed at Paramount, starting with Julia Crawford Ivers's adaptation of a play by Elsie Janis, *Nearly a Lady*, in which the playwright-actress starred:

1915: *Nearly a Lady, The Wild Olive*.

1916: HE FELL IN LOVE WITH HIS WIFE,[†] *Ben Blair, Pasquale, The American Beauty, Davy Crockett, The House of Lies, Her Father's Son, The Parson of Panamint, Redeeming Love, The Happiness of Three Women*.

1917: *Out of the Wreck, The World Apart, Big Timber, The Varmint, Jack and Jill,* TOM SAWYER, *The Spirit of '17*.

1918: *Huck and Tom, His Majesty Bunker Bean, Up the Road With Sallie, Mile-a-Minute Kendall, How Could You, Jean?,*[*] JOHANNA ENLISTS.[*]

[*] Starring Mary Pickford.
[†] Titles in SMALL CAPITALS are films known to have survived.

1919:   *Captain Kidd, Jr.,** *Anne of Green Gables.*†

1920:   HUCKLEBERRY FINN, *Judy of Rogue's Harbor,*† NURSE MARJORIE,† *Jenny Be Good,*† THE SOUL OF YOUTH, *The Furnace.*

1921:   THE WITCHING HOUR, *Sacred and Profane Love, Wealth, Beyond,* MORALS.

1922:   *The Green Temptation, The Top of New York.*

After the United States entered the war, Taylor directed Jack Pickford in *The Spirit of '17*. One critic wrote that "it radiates the splendid patriotism of the moment," calling it "an entertaining story of the United States in wartime," with young Pickford exposing the attempts of two German spies to blow up a mine. It seems to have been Taylor's answer to the antiwar (or, more accurately, anti-English) movie *The Spirit of '76*, which was regarded as pro-German propaganda and was seized under the wartime Espionage Act. All the film seems to have been guilty of was showing how badly the British redcoats, with the help of Indians, treated rebelling Americans during our Revolutionary War. The unfortunate man who wrote and produced it, Robert Goldstein, a costumer of German background who made a fortune from his investment in *The Birth of a Nation*, was sentenced to twelve years in prison and fined five thousand dollars. This strange story of wartime hysteria has been recorded in detail by Kevin Brownlow.‡

When Taylor renewed his Paramount contract for two years in November 1917, it was with the understanding that if he was accepted by the Canadian Army, the studio

* Starring Mary Pickford.

† Starring Mary Miles Minter.

‡ Kevin Brownlow, *The War, the West, and the Wilderness* (New York: Alfred A. Knopf, 1979), pp. 80–2.

would grant him leave for military service. He enlisted
the following July. Dr. H. M. Maddocks, president of the
British Overseas Club, who had been retained by the Canadian government as their examining physician for re-
cruiting, examined Taylor and described him as "a fine
physical specimen," though at forty-six the director was
an overage recruit. And it seems unlikely that Taylor's
eyesight had improved since his father's day.

Taylor enlisted as a private. He had his final checkup
in Chicago and on August 18, 1918, was shipped north-
east to Camp Fort Edward in Nova Scotia. His air of
authority and his ability as an experienced leader were
noticed; within two weeks he wore a lance corporal's
stripe. A week later he became corporal, and after five
weeks on the drill ground, sergeant. Three weeks in that
rank earned him the title of company sergeant major. It is
interesting that another noncommissioned officer at the
camp, Stuart Cooling, described Taylor as "a man never
thinking of himself, *always helping the underdog.*" After
four and a half months of training, Taylor sailed overseas
from Halifax with a troop of five hundred Canadian
soldiers. Their destination was Hounslow Barracks, west
of London, where they arrived on December 2, 1918. For
three weeks—since November 11—the war had been officially over. He spent only three days at Hounslow, with
the rank of acting regimental quartermaster sergeant,
after which he was transferred to the Expeditionary Force
Canteen near Victoria Station.

He was anxious to get to France before his discharge,
and he succeeded. His superiors were doubtless impressed
by his position as a Hollywood director ("He's the man
who directed Mary Pickford!") and his distinguished
family background (his father a major, his brother-in-

Captain Taylor in his Canadian Army uniform, 1918–19.

law an officer killed in action). He was made an officer when he was seconded to a lieutenancy in the Royal Army Service Corps, his number being F-58979. Among his belongings there was found an army pass issued at Dunkirk on April 4, 1919, granting Lieutenant Taylor leave. Continuing his quick rise up the ranks, he was promoted to captain in France. Before the month was out, he reached his final billet at Berguet: Major Taylor, Company D, 5th Battalion, Royal Fusiliers.

Punished in his youth, apparently for his inability to become a soldier, made to feel worthless, he had not only reached his father's military rank but had outdistanced him in worldly success. It was customary on discharge to revert to the next lower rank, so he left the army as Captain Taylor. He went back to his job at Famous Players–Lasky Paramount, arriving there on May 14, 1919. One week later, the Motion Picture Directors Association honored their president, returned from the wars, with a banquet at the Los Angeles Athletic Club.

Taylor's first movie assignment following his return was to direct Mary Miles Minter in *Anne of Green Gables*. Of the eight known surviving films directed by Taylor, the most important is *Huckleberry Finn* (1920). William K. Everson considers it "possibly still the best screen adaptation of Mark Twain." The script by Julia Crawford Ivers (whose father was Twain's friend), as well as her influence in the choice of a locale, endows the film with added authenticity. She had persuaded Taylor to take his company to Hannibal, Missouri, where Twain spent his boyhood. There is only one known copy of this *Huckleberry Finn* extant—in the film archives of the

George Eastman House in Rochester, New York, with subtitles in Danish.

The subtitles, though excessive, present no problem to a viewer familiar with Twain's text. It was a pleasure for me to reread the book before the screening. The most striking aspect of the film was the brilliant photography of James Van Trees. His sharp lighting and expert camera work show every face and object with a clarity that seems right for the story's time and place. The Ivers scenario opens with an actor playing Twain himself, writing in bed, while Huck, sitting on the edge of the bed, dictates his story.

The casting of Lewis Sargent as Huck, George Reed as Jim, and Frank Lanning as Huck's father seems inspired. Sargent is as tough and uncouth as a fifteen-year-old with corncob pipe and bad teeth should be. Reed's nobility of face and figure lend dignity to his role as the runaway slave. Lanning's drunken ferocity is startling: the scenes in which he beats up his son, realistically whaling his hide until the boy is unconscious, in a vain effort to get his hands on the stolen money, are among the most effective in the movie, along with the attack of delirium tremens in which he sees a lion in the log cabin. The Mississippi River and the surrounding landscape are well used, but not enough cinematic use is made of the raft moving on the water. Even when all the action is confined to the raft, it is usually moored to the shore.

The roles of the Duke and the King, the pair of thespian scoundrels who take over Huck's raft, swindle a theater audience, steal the Wilks money, and sell Jim into slavery, are character parts well acted by Orral Humphrey and Tom Bate. In the cameo role of poker-faced Johanna, Fay Lamport is perfect as the housewife watching Huck,

*Huck (Lewis Sargent) and his sadistic father (Frank Lanning)
in William Desmond Taylor's* Huckleberry Finn *(1920).*

in a girl's disguise, trying to thread a needle. A very young Esther Ralston not only plays angelic Mary Jane Wilks convincingly but appears in Huck's dream (a tableau scene) wearing a white gown and wings. Another charming use of tableau occurs during a Bible reading, when Huck daydreams about the pharaoh's daughter finding Moses in the bulrushes.

Everson has called the film "even in its abbreviated version . . . a superb piece of Americana." He detects signs that it was "drastically edited" by the studio at a time when exhibitors were complaining that movies were too long. It is true that several scenes are not allowed to develop as fully as they should. The worst flaw is the film's (or Paramount's) inability to rise completely above the racial prejudices of the period. Twain succeeded in his own era by his brilliant use of irony, but the movie interpolates unnecessary scenes of stereotypes—a little black girl eating watermelon and "darkies" dancing happily before their shanties. The movie oddly underplays Jim's tragedy. A crucial scene in the novel—Huck, against all his stated principles, passionately praying on his knees for Jim's safety—is presented briefly on the screen, as if it embarrassed Paramount and Taylor.

One thing that makes Twain's novel a masterpiece is its savage attack on racism. This is expressed by Huck, who *appears* to be favoring it. The film skirts this theme and tacks on a false ending, with Huck telling Mark Twain, seated in a rocking chair on a white-columned porch, of his love for Mary Jane Wilks. The novel's closing words— especially the last sentence—are too great to have been ignored in the film: "I reckon I got to light out for the Territory ahead of the rest, because Aunt Sally she's going to adopt me and sivilize me, and I can't stand it. I been there before."

Taylor, as a movie director, was a professional, a work-manlike and reliable craftsman who got the job done while keeping disruptive problems to a minimum—the kind of director most producers would prefer. Assuming he had the capacity to break out of the conventional mold, he either never had the opportunity to do so or chose not to. In the history of films, as in other arts, there have been only a few persons one would call great—from pioneers like Méliès, Griffith, and Chaplin to Kurosawa, Bergman, Orson Welles, and John Huston in more recent times. They usually, though not always, succeeded in doing what they (rather than some backer) wanted. William Desmond Taylor is an interesting figure for many reasons, but not for unusual creative qualities as a director.

7

Taylor's Household

IN THE spring of 1920, after the successful release of *Huckleberry Finn*, Taylor moved from the Los Angeles Athletic Club to Alvarado Court, on the recommendation of Douglas MacLean. The actor was one of the Taylor cronies who met regularly at the club. They included Arthur Hoyt, who acted in minor roles at Paramount and appeared in Taylor's last movie, *The Top of New York*; actor Antonio Moreno; directors Allan Dwan and James Kirkwood; Captain E. A. Salisbury, explorer and travel-film maker; and Marshall Neilan, one of the leading directors of the twenties. Gloria Swanson called them "the Mount Lowe Lodge group," referring to the California mountain resort where they went for drinking and cardplaying bouts and hunting expeditions.

Marshall Neilan (1891–1958) was a native Californian of Irish parentage, who had started out chauffeuring for Oliver Morosco and D. W. Griffith. By 1917, he had reached the top: Mary Pickford chose him to direct her in

Marshall Neilan (LEFT), *his wife, Blanche Sweet* (CENTER), *and Anita Stewart, the star of Metro's* In Old Kentucky *(1919), which Neilan directed.*

Rebecca of Sunnybrook Farm and Bret Harte's *M'liss.*
He married Blanche Sweet, whom he directed in *The
Sporting Venus* (1924) and Hardy's *Tess of the D'Urber-
villes* (1925).

Gloria Swanson in her memoirs acknowledged that she
and Neilan had had a torrid love affair. She said (in a
conversation at Sardi's, at which King Vidor and Colleen
Moore were also present) that "Mickey threw his career
away" by drinking and became bankrupt in 1933. Colleen Moore added: "Mickey was a genius who didn't grow
up until it was too late." When Blanche Sweet was asked
to describe Neilan, she said: "He was sensitive, creative,
and lots of fun, but he ruined his life with booze. That's
why I divorced him." Henry Peavey told the police that
only three people were frequent visitors at Alvarado
Court—Mabel Normand, Mary Miles Minter, and Marshall Neilan.

Neilan was a good friend of Normand and Minter, as
well as of Taylor. He was well aware of Mabel's drug
problem and remembered an ominous prediction, months
before the murder occurred, made by a federal drug agent
in Los Angeles. The agent told Neilan that Mabel, during
one of her visits to New York and Atlantic City, had got
mixed up with an East Coast drug ring. "Before she's
through," the agent told him, *"somebody's going to get
killed on her account."* (Italics added.)

Edward F. Sands is perhaps the strangest character of
all those involved in the Taylor case. Taylor, after moving to his new bungalow, hired Sands as cook and secretary, and Earl Tiffany as chauffeur. After the murder, the
police labeled Sands as Suspect No. 1, but their warrant
for his arrest cited larceny and burglary—there was no

Taylor and his custom-built McFarlan car, with chauffeur Harry Fellows (usually misidentified as Edward Sands), in 1920.

evidence for murder. Those who knew him, including Taylor, at first considered Sands to be a roly-poly, happy-go-lucky young man. He may have appeared so on the surface, but behind the facade there was a record of crime and military desertion of which Taylor and his friends were unaware. In 1921, Sands was twenty-seven. U.S. Navy records showed that he first enlisted in 1911, at age seventeen, giving his name as Edward Fitzgerald Snyder, his year of birth as 1894, his parents' names as Murray T. and Marguerite Snyder, and his place of birth as Marion, Ohio. He was court-martialed for embezzlement and sentenced to one year in Portsmouth Navy Yard Prison, after which he was dishonorably discharged.

During the war he reenlisted, again under his real name of Snyder, as a ship's cook at the New York Navy Yard. (Did the navy fail to check his record or, during wartime, decide he had paid for his youthful crime?) In January 1919, at New London, Connecticut, he became a deserter. A month later, adopting an alias, "Edward FitzStrathmore of Boston," he signed up with the navy for a third time, giving his age as twenty-four years ten months, his height as five feet, six and a half inches, and his weight as one hundred eighty-six pounds. His eye color was recorded as "the sixth shade of blue," his hair as brown, his complexion as ruddy.

Three months later, he again deserted. After six weeks, he joined the army. On May 19, 1919, he was assigned as a clerk in the finance department of the Army Depot at Columbus, Ohio. After passing a forged check, he deserted from the army in October 1919. All these facts, unearthed by the police after the murder, could not have been known to Paramount, who recommended "Edward F.

Sands" to Taylor as a good cook. The man Taylor hired as his chauffeur—a minor actor, Earl Tiffany, also recommended by the studio—was fired by Taylor for attempted blackmail eight months later and replaced by Howard Fellows.

Almost everyone seemed to find Sands likable, or at least amusing, including Mary Miles Minter. When she was asked whether she thought Sands murdered Taylor, she said, "Sands? No, he was just a fat, jolly Cockney [he affected a British accent]. He couldn't have done it." Neva Gerber revealed that Sands had been infatuated with a girl he met at Wilson's Dancing Academy, for whom he bought gifts, including expensive lingerie, on Taylor's charge account. Antonio Moreno denied the rumor that Sands was homosexual. On the contrary, he called Sands "girl crazy" and told King Vidor that "Sands jumped on anything in a skirt. Faith MacLean wouldn't let the man near her, and neither would Edna Purviance."

According to the Paramount art director George Hopkins, Taylor at first considered Sands "the most marvelous servant in the world." Hopkins himself thought Sands very clever but odd—"a Dickens character." Taylor showed Hopkins the strange parchment Sands had written in his fine penmanship, swearing "I am your slave for life," which amused the director. Others believed Sands was mentally unstable. A friend, George S. Brettner, told the police Sands suffered from bouts of depression and carried a .45 Colt revolver, threatening "to blow his head off when he reached age 35." Brettner thought him deranged.

As for the rumor the police allowed to circulate, that Sands was Taylor's missing brother Denis (who was forty-five in 1921), Antonio Moreno denied it categorically:

"Sands was a horse's ass. He was no relation. When Bill Taylor snapped his fingers, Sands jumped and did what he was told. He knew he had a cushy job and was terrified of losing it. He did everything to please Taylor, like writing that parchment, and waited for his big chance." The big chance came in the summer of 1921.

On May 5, 1921, Taylor underwent surgery, apparently for a stomach ulcer. It would seem that he recovered quickly: he was playing golf before the end of the month. His doctor advised him to get away from Hollywood for a while and recuperate abroad, so he booked passage on the *Mauretania*, sailing for England on June 9.

At Paramount, he had become friendly with Edward Knoblock, an American playwright and novelist who had begun his career in George Pierce Baker's drama workshop at Harvard. Knoblock, living in England during the war, became a British subject in 1916. *Kismet*, his most famous play, had been a hit in London as well as on Broadway, and Jesse Lasky hired him in 1920 to write scenarios at Paramount. Knoblock invited Taylor to make use of his elegant Albany apartment on Piccadilly during his London stay, and Taylor agreed to do so only if Knoblock moved into the Alvarado Court bungalow. Knoblock had just been hired by Douglas Fairbanks to write the script of *The Three Musketeers*, so the two friends agreed to swap apartments.

Before he left for England, Taylor, who was worried that something might be lacking for his guest during his absence, foolishly signed a blank check and instructed Sands to use it only in the case of emergency. During Taylor's absence, Sands filled in the figure of $5,000 and went to his employer's bank, explaining that his boss

Taylor (wearing eyeglasses) on set of Sacred and Profane Love, *in which he directed Elsie Ferguson, at his right. At left are author Somerset Maugham and playwright Edward Knoblock, who occupied Taylor's bungalow.*

wanted him to buy a new auto before his return. The signature was authentic, and the bank gave Sands the cash. Having become adept at copying Taylor's signature, Sands had no trouble cashing smaller sums on other forged checks. Taylor is described in Knoblock's memoirs as "a quiet, very sympathetic man," but the playwright himself "didn't like the look of Sands." His book contains one of the few firsthand accounts of what happened at Alvarado Court during Taylor's absence in England:

> I moved into [Taylor's] place—a pretty little two-story bungalow facing a court of several similar cottages surrounded by gardens. His servant's name was Sands. I didn't like the look of Sands, but he saw to me well enough. About a month after I had been there, Sands asked me if he could take off the last week before Taylor came back, as he was going to be married. He intended to go to the island of Catalina for his honeymoon, he said, and would be back in time for Taylor's return. Another servant he had found would take his place. I thought this reasonable enough and agreed. A huge trunk arrived in which Sands said he was going to pack the various household things he had collected for his "new little home." Sands left. But he didn't come back. Finally, a day before Taylor's return, I telephoned to the hotel in Catalina. Sands had never been there.

Taylor arrived from England the next day, and Knoblock met him at the station.

> We drove straight to his bungalow. He ran upstairs, opened his locked cupboard, and took out his cheque

book.... Sands had cashed a cheque for $5,000. ... Most of Taylor's wardrobe was gone, as well as dozens of little objects of value. My clothes and belongings Sands was clever enough not to touch, so as not to arouse my suspicions. By my giving him leave to go on a holiday, he had a clear start of a week. We decided he had probably gone to Mexico. He was never seen or found again.

After Taylor's murder, Knoblock said, "The suspicion fell on Sands. But I realized at once that a thief who had got safely away with a large amount of money and a trunkful of clothes would hardly return from Mexico to shoot a man, unless he wished to carry out an act of bitter vengeance."*

On August 3, 1921, Taylor swore out a complaint against Sands, informing Detective Sergeants Cline and Cato that he had been robbed of money, clothing, jewelry, and an auto, which was later found wrecked. When the police questioned Earl Tiffany about Sands, the ex-chauffeur said, "Sands read every letter that came into the house for Taylor." This was standard procedure for a secretary, and Taylor trusted his secretary implicitly. Sands had soon learned, from Ethel Daisy's letters, that Taylor's real name was Deane-Tanner.

After the murder, the newspapers printed a letter Ethel Daisy had written the previous autumn. She was now twenty, the same age as Mary Miles Minter, and she had seen her father in New York on his return from England. Her letter reveals only that she was a well-bred and loving daughter:

* Edward Knoblock, *Round the Room: An Autobiography* (London: Chapman and Hall, 1939), pp. 306–7.

Taylor's daughter, Ethel Daisy, circa 1922.

Dear Father of mine: I have read your letters over ever so many times until I almost know them by heart. I would have answered sooner only I have had a siege of infected fingers. Three, one right after the other, and have only gotten through with them. Of course, that made it rather difficult to draw [she studied at the Art Students League], so I stayed home a couple of days. I had one of the fingers cut four times but the others only once. Mercy goodness, I wish you didn't have to work so long. You'll wear yourself down again, so be careful, won't you, papa pettie dear? Will the picture with Miss Compson [*The Green Temptation*] be interesting? I do wish I might see you soon. I think of you so much it seems as if I saw you much more often than once in a while. I realize how seldom we really see each other and I surely do hope you'll be east again soon, dear. I'd like very much to send you some real nice things for Christmas but haven't the least idea what you'd like, so kindly tell me, please dear. I must stop now. Oh, Father dear, I do love you so much.

When the probate of Taylor's estate was filed, the public administrator listed Taylor's heirs as "unknown," but lawyers intervened on Ethel Daisy's behalf, showing that the will named Ethel Daisy Deane-Tanner of Mamaroneck, New York, as his sole legatee. Taylor's estate was at first estimated at $60,000. His tax consultant, Marjorie Berger, said that at his death he was preparing to pay income tax on substantial dividends from oil stocks, the certificates of which were missing. Examination of his check stubs, financial records, and other papers indicated that he possessed more money than was found. Mrs. Berger thought he might have rented a second safety-deposit box, but it was never located. In the end, his assets came to only $18,733, including $6,000 in the bank, $4,500 in government bonds, $5,000 in autos, $1,500 in jewelry, and $1,500 in household furnishings. For a well-paid director whose annual salary alone was $35,000—very high for the period—these assets are surprisingly low. Did Taylor spend the money on Mabel Normand, in the fight against her drug addiction and for her rehabilitation? A financial mystery was added to the other mysteries surrounding the Taylor case.

On Christmas Eve, 1921, greetings unexpectedly arrived in the mail from Sands, in the form of a note and two pawn tickets made out to "William C. Dene-Tanner." The pawn tickets were for Taylor's diamond cuff links, a gift from Mabel Normand, the most valuable piece of jewelry Sands had stolen. The note said: "Dear Mr. Taylor: So sorry to inconvenience you, even temporarily, also observe the lesson of the forced sale of assets. A merry Christmas and a prosperous New Year." It was signed, "Alias Jimmie Valentine," the name of an O. Henry story about a thief, which inspired a successful play, an MGM movie (1920), and a song that began: "Look out, look out for Jimmie Valentine, / For he's a pal of mine, / An educated crook."

The rumor that Sands was Taylor's brother persisted, until Mrs. Denis Deane-Tanner took steps to demolish it. She was appalled that her missing husband should be suspected of murder. She brought to the police a photo of Denis and samples of his handwriting. Denis was obviously much thinner and taller than Sands and at least twenty years older. The experts who compared their handwriting acknowledged that Edward Sands and Denis

Deane-Tanner could not be the same person. All they had in common was that they were both missing and were never found.

When District Attorney Thomas Lee Woolwine issued a warrant for Sands's arrest, six days after Taylor's murder, the police circulated this description:

> Edward F. Sands, American, about 26 years old, height 5 ft. 7 inches. Weight, rather heavy build, at one time 195 pounds, now believed 175–185 pounds but noticeably stout or heavy build. Round face, light complexion, hair brown and quite heavy and straight, not curly or wavy. Always rather bushy. Heavy eyebrows, short nose, peculiar looking mouth, when closed seems quite small. Usually well dressed; smokes cigarettes incessantly. Makes impression as well groomed, possibly like a foreigner. Slight trace of English or Canadian accent. Fine penmanship—formerly clerk or bookkeeper. Served in U.S. Navy; thought to have used several names.

The accompanying photo showed Sands as youthful, obese, round-faced, with slicked-down hair and eyebrows that almost met across his forehead; he wore a bow tie.

Not long after the murder, a letter purporting to come from Sands reached the district attorney: "I did not murder Taylor," it said, "but I know who did. I can untangle this murder mystery for you." The writer demanded immunity and police protection, and a message from the police was published in the newspapers promising both, provided that Sands could prove he did not commit the murder. The police were aware that the letter, whose writer carefully explained it had been dictated to a friend, was not in Sands's hand. When they had no response to

The strange photo of Edward Sands, military deserter, thief and forger, released by the police. It was retouched, probably by newspapers to help its reproduction, becoming almost worthless.

the guarantee of immunity, the police decided the letter was a hoax. They had already received almost three hundred "confessions" to the crime.

One of the many false trails pursued by the police involved the strange behavior of a newspaperman, H. C. Connette, formerly with the *Los Angeles Times* and the *Long Beach Press*. An alcoholic and a drug addict, Connette sailed for Hawaii right after the murder and was hired by the *Hilo Tribune*, for which he wrote an article suggesting that Taylor's killer was hiding in Hilo. "The slaying was of the vendetta type," he wrote, "and the man who did the killing did so from a revenge motive." He claimed Sands was innocent and the murder involved no women. The Hawaii police told Woolwine that Connette, in drunken conversation, had implied that Taylor was homosexual, also naming Gareth Hughes, a handsome movie actor featured in the title role of James M. Barrie's *Sentimental Tommy* (1921). Called into Woolwine's office, Hughes gave a satisfactory account of his whereabouts on the night of the murder and was released. Connette then circulated a statement that *he* had killed a man in defense of his honor, giving a detailed description of the room where Taylor was slain. Sent back to Los Angeles by the Hawaii police, he retracted this statement on arrival. They took him to the Taylor residence, where Faith MacLean confirmed that he was not the man she saw on February 1. It turned out that Connette was registered at a Turkish bath on Fourth Street at the time of the murder. He was released and the "Connette episode," like many others, ended.

The original arrest warrant for Sands cited larceny and burglary alone, but Sergeant Edward King now informed newsmen that formal charges of murder were about to be made, based on "new and conclusive evidence uncovered that day." Six or seven cigarette stubs had been found in the alleyway where the assassin had waited for his victim's return after Taylor took Mabel Normand to her car. The cigarettes were all from a special gold-tipped stock, custom-made for Taylor, which the chain-smoking Sands had used. "That just about proves Sands is the murderer," District Attorney Woolwine declared.

The *Los Angeles Examiner* had accused Woolwine of "erecting a barricade of silence between the searchers for truth and the truth itself." The president of the Northwest Association of Sheriffs and Police, Luke S. May, without mentioning Woolwine, criticized the handling of the case: "This case is no different from scores of others, except that the leading figures are more notable. Many more mysterious cases have been solved without publicity. The only difference is that in this case *some people don't seem to want the facts brought out,* and are withholding evidence." Woolwine, smarting from these criticisms, was boxed into the situation, and there seemed to be no way out of it.

Lawyer and author Thomas Lee Woolwine (1874–1925) was a native of Tennessee. He had joined the Los Angeles District Attorney's Office as a deputy in 1908 and captured public attention by crusading attacks against prostitution and liquor interests, which led to the first successful effort in the United States to recall a mayor—Arthur C. Harper of Los Angeles. Woolwine became the district attorney in 1914 and ran for governor of California in 1918; he was defeated by Hiram Johnson. In 1909, he had published a short romantic novel, *In the Valley of the Shadows*, the text of which was, oddly, printed on right-hand pages only.

Woolwine was well connected socially in the Hollywood community and was highly regarded as a speaker,

Mabel Normand, leaving the inquest, accompanied by District Attorney Thomas Lee Woolwine (LEFT) *and his deputy William C. Doran* (RIGHT).

with a host of friends in the studios, not only among the producers and performers but including such figures as William Desmond Taylor and Charlotte Shelby. He often appeared as an honored guest and speaker at studio banquets, such as the dinner Paramount gave for Roscoe Arbuckle before the scandal broke in 1921.

Sergeant Edward King, having had second thoughts about the implications of the newly found cigarettes, advised Woolwine to delay charging Sands with murder on that evidence alone. He pointed out that many of Taylor's friends, including actors and actresses, had been furnished with his cigarettes, which were known to be in abundant supply in Taylor's office. The cigarettes in themselves, he argued, proved nothing conclusively. There had been no mention of fingerprints being found on the half-smoked stubs on the lawn and in the alleyway. (Woolwine was also well aware that the police had bungled the detection of fingerprints in Taylor's rooms, having neglected to check for them the first day. When they got around to it, two days later, the numerous fingerprints of the detectives themselves made the evidence worthless.)

The murder warrant against Sands was never issued. His role in the case was nullified fifteen years later by Woolwine's successor, District Attorney Buron Fitts, who announced in 1937 that Sands was dead. He did not explain precisely when or where Sands's death had occurred or how he knew about it. In 1937, Sands would have been forty-three, years beyond the age at which he had vowed to end his life.

Henry Peavey, who succeeded Sands in the bungalow, was tall and heavyset rather than short and fat, like his predecessor. It is not clear whether Taylor knew when he hired him that Peavey was gay. If not, he learned it in

January 1922 when the Los Angeles police arrested Peavey on a charge of vagrancy and on allegations of indecent exposure in West Lake Park. Instead of firing him,
Taylor put up a bail bond, got him a lawyer, and was
scheduled to appear in court on his behalf the day after
the murder. Peavey's feelings of gratitude toward Taylor
and his genuine sorrow over his death became evident at
the inquest.

Even though the police decided, after severe questioning, that Peavey was not implicated in the murder, the
Hollywood correspondent of the New York *Daily News*,
Florabel Muir, one of the first reporters to reach the scene,
came to a private conclusion that Peavey was the murderer. In that era of ingenious women reporters, Muir
thought she could engineer a scoop by tricking Peavey
into a confession. She knew (from the movies) that blacks
were deathly afraid of ghosts. With the help of two confederates, Frank Carson and Al Weinshank, she offered
Peavey ten dollars if he would identify Taylor's grave
at the Hollywood Park Cemetery (which she had already
visited). Weinshank had gone on ahead with a white
sheet, and Muir and Carson drove Peavey to the site.

Weinshank, who came from a tough section of Chicago,
spoke in the accents of a hoodlum. When he loomed up in
his sheet and cried out, "I am the ghost of William Desmond Taylor. You murdered me. Confess, Peavey!"
Henry laughed out loud. Then he cursed them roundly.
Unfortunately for Muir, she was unaware that Taylor had
a distinctive British accent. Weinshank, as Muir revealed
in her memoirs,* not only spoke like a hoodlum but was
one of the Chicago mobsters who later were gunned down
in the famous St. Valentine's Day massacre.

* Florabel Muir, *Headline Happy* (New York: Henry Holt, 1950),
pp. 100–2.

Seven years later, Henry Peavey made the headlines again, when H. W. Friend Richardson, during the California gubernatorial campaign, claimed he had evidence that a famous actress had murdered Taylor. Peavey, living in Sacramento, was besieged by reporters to confirm this. Though he revealed that the police in 1922 had told him in no uncertain terms to get out of Los Angeles, he denied that he knew anything about the murderer. In 1931, Peavey died of paresis in a Monrovia hospital.

Rumors that Taylor himself was homosexual surrounded the case from the start, but no convincing evidence of it was ever presented. His past life, his many liaisons with women, his marriage at twenty-nine to Ethel May, his rendezvous with the blond beauty in the Adirondacks hotel, his banjo-playing "sister" in the Yukon, his engagement to Neva Gerber, and his devotion to Mabel Normand all indicate his heterosexuality. His close association with male companions with tastes similar to his own reinforces this conclusion. Only the Paramount art director George Hopkins, who was an acknowledged homosexual himself, implied that Taylor was of similar persuasion—he hinted they were lovers—but his side of the story surfaced after Taylor was no longer around. To some, the presence of oddball Edward Sands and gay Henry Peavey in the household gave support to Hopkins's allegation; others subscribed to guilt by association on the ground that Taylor was photographed with Somerset Maugham and Hugh Walpole.

Neither Gloria Swanson nor Blanche Sweet, who knew him, thought Taylor was homosexual. King Vidor, who did not know him and did know Hopkins, was not sure. Swanson, talking about Taylor on the occasion of the pub-

Paramount art director George Hopkins (LEFT) on the set of Morals,
starring May McAvoy (CENTER), which Taylor (RIGHT) directed late in 1921.

lication of her memoirs, startled some of us by saying, "One should never jump to conclusions. Wouldn't you have thought that Winston Churchill was heterosexual?" We admitted we did think so. "Well, read about him in that new biography of Somerset Maugham. Not that it proves anything, but it amazed me." The book revealed that Churchill told Maugham he went to bed with a man once "to see what it was like,"* the period being World War I and the man being actor Ivor Novello, the protégé of Churchill's private secretary, Edward Marsh. If it proved nothing, as Swanson thought, it did come as a surprise. As for Taylor, from the available evidence it seems likely that he (like Churchill) was heterosexual.

No consideration of the Taylor case can ignore the puzzling aspects of his life and character—his mysterious past, his love affairs, his interest in and fight against drugs, his amazing tolerance of untrustworthy characters, his periods of black depression, the desertion of his family, his wacky household, his generosity on the one hand and, on the other, the surprisingly diminished estate he left the daughter he obviously loved. These facts have provided many false leads and led to absurd "solutions" of his murder. The revelations of his past life, becoming known piecemeal following the murder, led some reporters to view him as a dissolute and corrupt type. Even his changed name was looked on as sinister. The testimony of the people closest to him, in all of whom he aroused admiration and love, alters the picture. Though he was no saint, he may have been something of a hero.

It is true that Taylor was too permissive and trusting and, in the case of Sands, foolish. His early hardships and

* Ted Morgan, *Maugham* (New York: Simon & Schuster, 1980), p. 152.

struggles may explain the fact that he was unusually generous and helpful to others. One could even argue that his anti-drug fight was absolutely foolish, since it cost him his life. But in no way is it discreditable; it was the price a romantic idealist would be prepared to pay.

The name of actress Claire Windsor surfaced in accounts of the Taylor murder, after she boasted to a reporter for the *Los Angeles Examiner* that she had been Taylor's guest at the Cocoanut Grove nightclub (in the new Ambassador hotel) only a week before his death. She remembered it as an enjoyable evening, except that Taylor mentioned his trouble with Sands and vowed to kill him if he turned up. Windsor, who mastered the art of publicity soon after her arrival in Hollywood, had come a long way from Cawker City, Kansas, where she had been born Olga Cronk. After inventing a more euphonious name for herself, she was frequently seen, and photographed, with Charlie Chaplin. Her more cautious mother, who took care of her child, sensed danger in the Taylor case; she told reporters that this had been Claire's first and only date with Taylor. In later versions of the story, the actress claimed she had in fact gone to the nightclub with Tony Moreno, where she met Taylor escorting a blonde she could not identify. But Moreno said *he* had escorted beautiful Betty Francisco, whom Taylor had directed in *The Furnace* (1920), and had joined parties with Taylor and Windsor. He said the couple left together. Fortunately for the former Olga Cronk, it was established that on the day of the murder Marshall Neilan had directed her on location with Richard Dix in *Fools First*. Claire Windsor's inconsequential role in the case did not deter her from talking about it authoritatively for years.

8

Mary Miles Minter

NEWS OF Taylor's murder, though it spread quickly after his body was discovered early on the morning of February 2, did not reach Mary Miles Minter until shortly after 11 a.m. When Carl Stockdale, an actor who heard the news on the set of *Suzanna*, phoned, he learned from her mother that she was not at home. Stockdale later told the police he had been visiting Mrs. Shelby between seven and nine the previous night, thereby providing Mary's mother with an alibi.

Mrs. Shelby was thunderstruck by the news. Without revealing where Mary was, she said she wanted to deliver the traumatic news to her daughter in person. Mary and her older sister, Margaret, were with their grandmother, Julia Branch Miles, where they had spent the previous night. Charlotte Shelby now headed to this house. Significantly, Mary always called her grandmother, whom she loved, "Mama" and Charlotte Shelby, whom she hated, "Mother."

Mary has recorded in detail how the news of Taylor's

death reached her. A long statement—"the first I have ever given under my own name"—appeared on August 15, 1923, in the *Los Angeles Times*, "the only newspaper which has not hounded me day and night with questions, questions, questions about Mr. Taylor." This is her account:

"It was about 11 o'clock [on the morning of February 2, 1922]. I was standing in my undergarments before the mirror, fixing my hair. I heard Mother's footsteps coming pat, pat, pat down the hall. I knew something was wrong by the way she was walking. She pounded on my door." Her mother always scolded her for appearing in a negligee, and when Mary called out that she was dressing, Charlotte shouted: "Let me in, or I'll break down the door."

When Mary opened it, she found her mother greatly excited. "What do you think has happened?" said Charlotte. "William Desmond Taylor has just been found murdered in his bed!"

Mary said nothing, while her mother

> talked on and on in a most excited manner: I can't remember all she said, but it was something like this would teach me a lesson as to how to behave in the future. Then she said, "Well, why don't you say something?" I couldn't. I was too hurt.
>
> I grabbed a hat, a wrap, and then I began to look through my pocketbook and the drawers of the dresser. I was hunting for the keys to my car. I thought I would go frantic.
>
> "Where are you going?" Mother asked.
>
> "To him, of course."
>
> "No, you cannot. I shall not let you!" she said and stood before the door to stop me.

"You've kept me from the man I love in life, and
you can't keep me from him in death. I'm going to
him if I have to throttle you to get past," I cried. And
she stepped aside.

Mary said she drove "in a daze" to Taylor's house.
The afternoon edition of the *Los Angeles Record* reported
her arrival at Alvarado Court, where the police recognized her and felt sympathy for her genuine distress,
which she made no effort to hide:

> Tears streaming down her pretty face, Mary Miles
> Minter, famous motion picture star, hurried to the
> door of the Taylor bungalow at noon today and asked
> brokenly, "It isn't true, is it?" Detective Sergeant
> Wallis said, "Taylor is dead." "Oh my God, I can't
> believe it," Miss Minter cried out with a gesture of
> despair.

Sergeant Wallis explained to her that she could not see
the body, because the coroner had removed it to the undertaker's. No one could now enter the house, which the police had sealed. Rushing back to her car, she drove "round
and round downtown" until she located Ivy Overholtzer's
mortuary at Tenth and Hill streets.

Informed again that she could not see the body—at that
moment, the coroner was "trying to find the bullet"—she
sobbed, "I *must* see him, I *must* see him." They told her
it was against the law to allow anyone to see the body
prior to the inquest. She would not leave; this was Hollywood, and she was a star. She was finally told she could
see the body the next day at noon, even though the coroner's inquest was two days off.

Mary was still "too frantic" to return home. She drove

to Mabel Normand's and, ignoring the reporters waiting downstairs, rushed up to the bedroom and confronted Mabel. Some accounts claimed that they went into the bathroom and opened all the faucets so that the running water would cover their voices. Mary Miles Minter said that she "grasped Mabel by the shoulders, shook her, and looked straight into her eyes. 'What do you know about it?' I asked. 'Nothing,' she replied simply, 'not a thing, but what they have told me.' And I believed her, and still believe her."

Late that day, Mary had to endure an interview with a reporter from the *Record* in her mother's presence. "No, I never was engaged to William Desmond Taylor, I regret to say," she stated. "No, I was not at his home on the night he was murdered. I was at mama's house, reading a book. I always call grandma 'mama' and mother 'mother.' I loved him—of course not as—well, you know—but I loved him devotedly. He looked upon me more or less as a child, don't you know. And although I saw a great deal of him before I went to Europe, after we got back we couldn't drag him away from his work, could we, mother?"

"No," said Mrs. Charlotte Shelby, "he was a hard worker. Really, he was more interested in his business than anything else."

"Do you know where his ex-wife and daughter are?" the reporter cruelly asked Mary.

"Why, he had no wife! He was never married, I'm positive of that."

"But maybe, Mary, he didn't tell you he was married," her mother broke in.

"But mother, I knew him so well—I am sure he wasn't married. I was never engaged to marry him—no, it wouldn't be fair to say that I was. Of course, every once in a while someone has me engaged to someone—they've had me engaged to eight men so far. You see, he was nearly 50 years old—although I loved him and would have even if he was 75—but oh no, there was nothing to that."

"Had you heard of a romance between Mabel Normand and Mr. Taylor?"

"No, I hadn't but I don't think there was anything to that. I love little Mabel Normand. She is big-hearted and I appreciate her sterling qualities."

The next day, Mary could hardly wait for noon to arrive, and she left the house in good time without informing her mother of her plans. At last she reached Overholtzer's and was allowed to see Taylor's body.

They let me in all alone with him. I pulled back the sheet and looked at him. But he was not the same. His skin was waxen. I leaned down and put my arms about him, my cheek to his. His face was cold, so cold, but not a cold like ice.

"Do you love me, Desmond?" I said.

He answered me. I could hear his voice. "I love you, Mary. I shall love you always," he whispered.

I kissed him and put a red rose in his hands from a bouquet I had brought. The door opened. The undertaker was there. I went away.

Soon after this encounter, the first issue of *The American Mercury*, edited by H. L. Mencken and George Jean Nathan, came out. It printed Mary Miles Minter's account of her visit with Taylor under the heading "Metaphysics of the Movies."

Mary Miles Minter was sixteen and Taylor was forty-seven when they met for the first time. This was in 1919, after Taylor's return from the war, when Paramount assigned him to direct her in *Anne of Green Gables*. It is hard to believe that this teenager already had thirty-four films and a stage career to her credit, but she had started on Broadway at age six, under Charles Frohman's management, as "Little Juliet Shelby." She had been born Juliet Reilly in 1902, but her mother (born Lily Pearl Miles) changed their name to Shelby after leaving her husband, J. Homer Reilly of Texas. Guided by her mother's determined hand, Juliet, endowed with charm and blond prettiness, had her first great stage success in *The Littlest Rebel*, with William and Dustin Farnum.

The watchful Gerry Society—which policed all stage performers under sixteen to ensure that they were not victims of parental abuse or exploitation and were getting an education—caused Charlotte Shelby to seek an older identity for Little Juliet, who of course did not attend school. Charlotte's older sister, Mrs. Minter, had been killed in an accident with her daughter, Mary Miles Minter, and Charlotte illegally appropriated her niece's birth certificate to provide Juliet with a new name and age.

Recalling her mother's exploitation of her childhood, Mary wrote with bitterness that when she reached seventeen, "My mother tried to keep me a 'little girl' with curls down my back, but earlier she made me appear and act older than I was. When I was eight, I was passed off for sixteen, twice my age, and dressed as a midget, with high heels and long skirts, so that I could play the stellar role

in *The Littlest Rebel* at the Chicago Opera House. . . .
These things have an effect upon a child that all the training and coaching in the world cannot eliminate."

As soon as Charlotte learned that much more money
could be made in the movies than on the stage, the four
women—mother, sister, grandmother, and the littlest
rebel—headed for Hollywood. Mrs. Shelby negotiated a
contract with Metro for a series of six Mary Miles Minter
films. A full-page ad in the *Motion Picture News* of July
31, 1915, announced "filmdom's newest sensation—the
premier juvenile star, little Mary Miles Minter." One
reviewer said that in *Emmy of Stork's Nest*, her second
film in the series, Mary had "graduated from straight
child parts into characters that permit her to play a child
and a young woman in the same picture, and she does it
exceedingly well." Her third Metro movie, *Barbara Friet-*
chie, got even better notices, and rival producers began
to make her offers. After she completed her sixth film,
Sally in Our Alley, Mrs. Shelby refused to renew the
Metro contract. The enraged Louis B. Mayer trashed the
last film, incorporating part of it into an inferior movie
in an ineffective act of revenge.

Mrs. Shelby negotiated much better terms with the
American Film Company at Santa Barbara, insisting on
the important provision that they bill Mary as their number one star. Her films did consistently well at the box
office, but were they any good? There is the testimony of
Edward Wagenknecht, a trustworthy historian of silent
films, whose book has the virtue of having been written
from personal experience—he *saw* these films: "The saccharine vehicles in which [Mary Miles Minter] was generally presented all too seldom afforded opportunities for
acting. She herself was not saccharine, however; she was

Young Mary Miles Minter and staff in her "publicity office" at Metro Pictures. Her mother, Mrs. Shelby, is seated (CENTER). *Mary and her sister Margaret* (RIGHT) *play amidst the Minter stills on the floor.*

Lunch break on location for Anne of Green Gables *(1919). Minter front center, of course.*

a golden, peaches-and-cream kind of girl, in whom all the sweet, innocent charms of youth were embodied."* On the other hand, Edward Sloman, who directed *The Ghost of Rosy Taylor*, one of Mary's two films to have survived (the other is *The Eyes of Julia Deep*), told Kevin Brownlow, "I didn't like the story, and I didn't like the star. Mary Miles Minter was quite young then—sixteen—and very beautiful. Without doubt, she was the best-looking youngster I ever saw, and the lousiest actress." Mary herself might well have agreed, judging from some of her remarks to interviewers. She disliked most of the stories they assigned to her and did not consider herself a good actress. "I'm making pictures because, by making them, I can make money," she told one writer. "I ought not to say this, but it is the truth. I hate all this talk about my art. *'My art, my art!'* Always 'my art,' when what they really mean is 'my money.' "

The chance for really big money came in 1918, when the contract with American was completed. Paramount had just lost Mary Pickford, the most successful movie actress in the business, and Adolph Zukor thought he saw a chance to build Mary Miles Minter into a star of such magnitude that she would equal, if not outshine, America's sweetheart. In that year, Mrs. Shelby, her daughter's legal guardian—Mary was still a minor—reached her pinnacle.

She made Paramount guarantee a total income of $1.3 million over five years. In return, the young star was committed to making twenty films, but this was no great problem: she had just made twenty-six films in four years. The new contract was the talk of Hollywood: Mary would

* Edward Wagenknecht, *The Movies in the Age of Innocence* (Norman: University of Oklahoma Press, 1962), pp. 233–4.

get $50,000 each for the first five films; $60,000 each for the second five; $70,000 each for the third five; and $80,000 each for the last five. She completed eighteen of the twenty before she retired in the wake of the Taylor scandal. Paramount owed her $160,000 for the two unmade films, but Mrs. Shelby made them settle for $350,000 in cash. She felt financially triumphant, of course, but she made a mistake. Paramount wanted Mary in one more role, the female lead in *The Covered Wagon*, which Mrs. Shelby instantly vetoed. A western for Mary Miles Minter—not on your life! It made film history as the first big classic movie about pioneering in the Old West, and it also made a star of the little-known Lois Wilson, who happily substituted for Mary. If Mrs. Shelby had consented, it might have saved Mary's film career.

Mrs. Shelby's other misfortune, one beyond her control, was that her time had almost run out. Mary Miles Minter was coming of age; on her twenty-first birthday, in April 1923, she would no longer be subject to her mother's legal control.

In her own inimitable style, Mary recorded in the *Los Angeles Times* the story of her one true love, William Desmond Taylor, revealing how much she thought he loved her. His first words to her, which could not have been more conventional, impressed her deeply:

> "How do you do, Miss Minter?" he said to me when first we were introduced, and then he smiled. Always before I had been called Mary and treated like a child by men and women alike, but Mr. Taylor called me "Miss Minter," which at that age [sixteen], heart hungry as I was, made an instant impression....

I knew when I laid eyes on him that he was the one man in the world for me, and that he reciprocated my love. It was not long afterward that we were in New England, making a picture [*Anne of Green Gables*]. My mother, my grandmother and my sister were with the company. I used to listen for his footsteps as he came into the door of our little hotel where we stayed. I recognized them as they went up the stairway into his room. . . .

One time, it was my seventeenth birthday, we all went into Boston for a dinner party for me. He rode in the automobile between my grandmother and me. The road was rough and bumpy, his arms were spread across the rear of the back seat in which we rode. One bump threw grandmother against him and he said, "I guess I will have to hold you." But his arm did not embrace me.

"Dare I, dare I?" I said to myself. I dared, and I reached up at his coat sleeve until he dropped his arm about my waist. The thrill of that innocent act thrilled me for days and days. We spent what little time we could together, which was not much because mother always watched. Every night after I had gone to bed, she used to sit in the little parlor with him just as much as he would let her, while he was working on his script.

One day it rained dreadfully. We were out somewhere and he wrapped his coat about me and took me to the hotel. There stood mother, fairly raging. She accused Mr. Taylor before the entire company of taking me out, humiliating him most shamefully. For two days I hardly spoke to him and then I apologized for mother's action. "Your mother is right, Mary," he said. "She is right and you must always obey her."

That was the beginning of quarrels between mother and I. He soon left and came to California. Grandmother and I came later, while mother and sister remained in the East. Sister Margaret had a sort of beaked nose and she had it operated on to straighten it out. . . .

Until she knew of my love for Mr. Taylor, mother had only words of praise for him. Then suddenly she turned against him. I told Mr. Taylor of her attitude. "Your mother knows best, Mary. I am an old man," he would say, but he was not old in spirit or understanding and that was all that mattered to me. He was mine. I wanted him, to be his wife, to be able to do the thousand and one little things for him that only a wife can do. I would have married him then and there, but he said we must wait. . . .

But I did not want to wait. Perhaps many women would be ashamed to admit what I have admitted. But I am not ashamed. Our love was a glorious thing. "Why should we wait?" I would protest. Then I wrote letters, passionate, impulsive letters. Some of them were published. Many of those letters were written two years before he died. And he kept them. That was my one thought at the time: he kept them. Surely he must have loved me deeply, sincerely, to have kept them for so long.

We were never engaged in the sense that he asked me to marry him. . . . Finally, he told me I must not write him any more and must not call him up, that he would telephone me. I waited a week, two weeks, three weeks and he did not call. I swallowed my

Appearance and Reality: *Together on the set of* Judy of Rogue's Harbor *(1920),*
Taylor (holding mistletoe) and Minter pretend that she is in love with young
actor Alan Sears, when they both know she adores Taylor.

humiliation and called him. His butler [Peavey] answered and told me he was ill. He was too ill to talk to me. I gave the butler instructions of what to make him eat, to see that he was well covered during the night. For five days he did not eat a thing, and during it all I suffered more than I can express. . . .

Early in December [1921], before he was shot, I had telephoned him that I must see him. We would pass on the lot and he would smile so sweetly, but in his eyes was the love-light that none but I could see. He made an appointment for me to come to his house in two weeks. Grandmother and I went. The house was dark. I was heartbroken. In the keyhole I twisted one of the little golden hairpins that I wear so that he would know I was there.

No word from him, no telephone call. On December 23 I was downtown buying some Christmas presents—one for him that I never got to give him, I have it still. There in the store opposite me in another aisle he stood. He smiled so sweetly, bowed and was gone. The clerk brought something and I told her to wrap it up. I don't even know what it was, I was so dazed.

Though her account gives December as the date of their last encounter, the police learned that she had visited him on January 30, two nights before his murder. Their source of information was Arthur Hoyt, Taylor's close friend and associate at the Athletic Club. Hoyt told the police that he called on Taylor at the bungalow around 6:00 p.m. on January 31 and found him sitting at his desk, looking extremely worried. When Hoyt asked what the trouble was, Taylor swore him to secrecy before explaining.

On the previous night, quite late—1:00 or 2:00 a.m.—
he had had a visit from "the sweetest, most adorable
young lady in the world." She was madly in love with
him, though he was old enough to be her father. Hoyt
guessed that the caller was Mary Miles Minter, and Taylor said yes, she had come alone to his rooms, hoping to
spend the night with him. He had great difficulty in finally
persuading her to let him take her home.

Mary was unaware that the police had found three
blond hairs on Taylor's coat. From samples collected
from the combs and hairbrushes in her studio dressing
room, they ascertained that the hairs were hers. After the
murder, Mary, summoned by Deputy District Attorney
William C. Doran, arrived at his office with her attorney,
John G. Mott. Told that Peavey said she had visited Taylor two nights before the murder, she replied, "Peavey is
lying. I have not seen Mr. Taylor for several months."
Then they explained that three of her hairs were found on
the coat he was wearing when he was murdered, and she
fell silent. The truth finally emerged.

On the night of January 30, she told her grandmother
that she could no longer bear Taylor's silence. She had
made up her mind to deliver in person a note she had just
written: "Dear William Desmond Taylor: This is goodbye. I want you to know that I will always love you.
Mary." She said she arrived at his apartment sometime
after midnight, gave him the letter, and stayed forty minutes. He told her she should not have come; he also had
written a farewell note, which he hadn't yet mailed her.
She said he was trembling and that he repeated to her
what he had said two months earlier: "Mary, to me you
are the morning sun, bright, beautiful and with the future
before you, and my sun is already setting. Don't you see,

my dear, I simply cannot allow you to sacrifice yourself for a man of my age."

If he was trembling, it may have been from fear rather than (or perhaps as well as) attraction. As nicely as he could, he was trying to put an end to a relationship potentially dangerous for both of them and impossible from his view, while she was wholly intent on a love affair.

It is interesting that her statement to the police in no way implicated her mother. On the contrary, if Charlotte Shelby knew the real truth, she was well aware that Mary's relationship with Taylor—such as it was—had been over since December. If she previously had a motive to kill Taylor, Mrs. Shelby no longer had one. The farewell late-night visit of January 30 only confirmed the end of the affair.

Mary's release from her bondage to her mother became legal on April 25, 1923. Her hatred of acting, her wish to retire from the screen, and the murder of Taylor all seemed to have a liberating effect on her repressed and controlled life. Her tongue had become even freer than before, and she reveled in its use.

Regarding the inscription on her photo, she stated: "I never even called him 'Bill' in my life. The man was too wonderful for that. I don't care what anybody says, or what they prove against him, I know he was the finest thing in the world."

And she gloried in explaining her great love for Taylor: "It was just a beautiful thing that seldom occurs in the world today as I see it, as it is forced upon me. It was simply a beautiful white flame. I had always been a reserved, very retiring girl, and he was the first man and the only man who ever embodied all the glories of manhood in one private body. . . . I had always known that this was

151

The classic beauty of Mary Miles Minter.

just an exquisite chapter in my life that must necessarily
be a brief one. I couldn't bear to part with it."

Mary apparently also wrote out a long reverie about
Taylor one day on the set, when he was directing her in
one of her movies. She employed an easily decipherable
schoolgirl code of dots, circles, squares, triangles, and
other figures. The original and the decoded text were
widely reproduced in the papers:

What shall I call you, you wonderful man? You
are standing on this lot, the idol of an adoring company. You have just come over and put your coat on
my chair. I want to go away with you, up to the hills
or anywhere so we'd be alone—all alone in a beautiful woodland lodge. You'd be cook (as I can only
make tea) and fetch the water and build the fire.

Wouldn't it be glorious to sit in a big comfy couch,
by a cozy warm fire, with the wind whistling outside,
trying to harmonize with the faint sweet strains of
music coming from our phonograph. And then you'd
have to get up and take off the record. . . . Did you
really suppose that I intended you to take care of
me like a baby?

Oh no, for this is my part. I'd sweep and dust (they
make the sweetest little dust caps, you know) and tie
fresh ribbons on the snowy white curtains and feed
the birds and fix the flowers, and oh, yes, set the
table and help you with the dishes and then in my
spare time I'd darn your socks.

I'd go to my room and put on something soft and
flowing. Then I'd lie on the couch and wait for you.
I might fall asleep, for a fire always makes me
drowsy—then I'd wake to find two strong arms

around me and two dear lips pressing on mine in a long sweet kiss.

This, too, was found in a book on Taylor's shelves. How could the public, given such intimate glimpses, not believe that Taylor was a lecher who deserved what he got?

Shortly after she turned twenty-one, Mary Miles Minter left her mother's house for good. She then engaged an attorney, Neil McCarthy, to start a suit against Charlotte Shelby for an accounting of one million dollars. Charlotte immediately took to her sickbed, and Mary talked volubly to reporters:

> They never would let me be a girl, to do the things that other girls do. I never had the chance to play tag, or hide-and-go-seek, or have a kiddie-car. I was always petted and pampered, tutored and touted, made to believe I was something I was not, do things I did not want to do, say things I did not mean. From morning to night I had money, money, money talked and preached to me. I have earned lots of it, fairly hate it, and have none of it. . . . When I was a baby, just four years old, they took me away from my home and my daddy. We went to New York and mother accepted a theatrical engagement. Soon afterward I was given a part on the stage, and ever since mother's work has consisted of drawing my salary.
>
> The power of money was drilled into me on every hand. Mother said, "Be powerful even if you have to walk across the graves of others to get it." She has no sympathy for the misfortune of another. She is her own best press agent, and knows what to say to create sympathy for herself. My sister Margaret is

a yes-girl. It's yes mama, this and yes mama, that. ...

I have left home to be alone, to get away from the constant argument, from the posing, the nagging, the humiliation of being told that I myself have never done anything, would not have anything, had it not been for the watchful eye of mother and Margaret, my older sister, three years older than I.

My mother is not in danger of death. It's only a ruse to get me to call off the lawsuit. Yes, mother and Margaret say they love me, that I am the very life and breath of their existence. They should have said "I have been" all of that, and I was—for where would either be without the money I have made? How can my mother expect me to love and obey her when I have seen the way she has treated her own mother for years, as a glorified servant?

Asked if she'd make up with her family and go back, she said, "Go back? Not if I have to scrub floors first. I'm through. I'm going to live my own life."

The public quarrels of Mary, her mother, and Margaret provided the newspapers with a steady stream of copy throughout the twenties and thirties. Brief reconciliations were followed by breakups; family ruptures would be healed, only to recur. Even Margaret—her mother's favorite, according to Mary—engaged in financial fights with Charlotte. Margaret had married Hugh Hamilton Fillmore, grandson of President Millard Fillmore, but the marriage did not last, and Margaret took to drink. Her mother, alarmed by Margaret's lawsuits and her generally erratic behavior, tried to have her committed to a mental institution. At one point, when the court awarded Margaret a judgment of twenty thousand dollars and assigned her mother's fashionable home at Laguna Beach as settlement, Margaret forced Charlotte out of the house, ordering her furniture and possessions put on the sidewalk. At once Mrs. Shelby summoned press photographers. She posed forlornly amid her belongings to expose to the world her daughter's cruelty.

Mary had also been awarded money, and she moved to New York, where she took an apartment on Central Park South. In 1925, her beloved grandmother Julia Branch Miles became terminally ill with cancer in Los Angeles. The World War I ace Eddie Rickenbacker offered to fly Mary to California, but storms prevented him from getting clearance; Mrs. Miles died before they could take off.

Leonard Sillman, the Broadway producer of *New Faces*, gives a firsthand account of the new Mary, overweight and overdramatic, throwing a party in Manhattan in the late twenties:

> The door was opened to us by a vision of loveliness, Miss Minter herself. She was still the proud owner of one of those supremely beautiful faces the silent screen seemed to breed, but her loveliness stopped at her neckline. That fabulous face now bloomed atop one of the widest, roundest, most barrel-like bodies ever created. All through her movie career, Mary's mother had kept her on a starvation diet. Her career over, Mary decided she would make up for all those lost meals and had been on an eating spree ever since. "How do you do, dear boy," she said to me, "bravo, bravo, bravo!" I said I was delighted to meet her because I had always been one of her devoted fans. She gave me a withering look and said, "Don't *ever* discuss my career, bravo!"

Later that evening, Sillman said, she "marched to the middle of the room, put her hand to her throat and screamed, 'Each man kills the thing he loves!' and dropped in a faint." At another party, where Glenn Hunter, the popular young actor who had created *Merton of the Movies*, was also a guest, Mary said to him, "I hear you're a very good actor. Get up and recite, bravo!" Hunter replied that he never did recitations, and she became violent. "Up! Up on your feet! Recite, recite!" She was so loud and insistent that poor Hunter stood up and sang "Spring Is Here" from the current musical, after which they all applauded—except Mary, who said, "Worst singing I ever heard."*

After her grandmother's death, Mary moved abroad and lived in Paris. Her mother joined her there, temporarily reconciled. (Did Mary have an illegitimate daughter by an unknown father early in 1929? After her death in 1984, a blond housewife from Santa Monica, Margaret Kozma, swore that Mary Miles Minter gave birth to her in Paris and that she was farmed out as an infant to Hungarian parents by Mrs. Shelby. The case was being heard in California courts in 1989.) After their return to New York at the end of 1929, Charlotte and Mary quarreled again and separated. Late that year, Buron Fitts, the new Los Angeles district attorney, reopened the unsolved Taylor case, and the rumor spread that Charlotte Shelby would be indicted for Taylor's murder.

Charlotte acted decisively. She had her attorney release to the *Los Angeles Examiner* the appeal she had sent to Buron Fitts, demanding complete exoneration of any complicity in the murder of Taylor. "I am desirous of a full

* Leonard Sillman, *Here Lies Leonard Sillman* (New York: Citadel Press, 1959), pp. 66–7.

Mrs. Shelby and her famous daughter, circa 1921.

investigation and vindication of my name," her statement said, "to stop the circulation of insinuations that have repeatedly been made that I am implicated." On the day after Christmas, she released a second statement:

"I am a woman who has always stood alone. I was not in love with William Desmond Taylor. I was not in love with anyone. And no one was in love with me. I never held a purely social conversation with Mr. Taylor in my life. He was always aloof, a man of mystery, polished, distant and reserved. For years there have been malicious innuendos and rumors against me. I did not kill William Desmond Taylor. I do not know who did kill him. I demand a complete exoneration, or an indictment for murder." Buron Fitts finally agreed to meet with her at her attorney's home. He acknowledged that there was no evidence for an indictment, and Mrs. Shelby told the press she was satisfied.

She filed suit in 1932 against her broker, Leslie B. Henry, charging he had speculated with Mary's money and had lost $450,000 of it. A bitter case, it was fought in the courts for years, with Mrs. Shelby claiming Henry had tried to blackmail her into silence by threats of her involvement in the Taylor case. Leslie Henry was found guilty. He spent three years in prison, and actual settlement of the finances dragged on for nearly three decades.

Margaret Shelby Fillmore died in 1939, completely alcoholic and virtually friendless. Mother Shelby, now fully reconciled to Mary, lived with her younger daughter in Santa Monica until her death in 1957, at age eighty-five. Hedda Hopper reported that "Mary Miles Minter, 55, star of silent films, acknowledged yesterday that she planned to be married, but said that the death of her mother had caused postponement." Later that year, Mary became the wife of an American of Danish extraction, Brandon O. Hildebrandt, her partner for many years in a number of real estate and other business ventures. To please his wife, who was obsessed with numerology, he changed his name to O'Hildebrandt. He died in 1965.

Mary continued to live in Santa Monica for almost twenty years, the longest survivor of the Taylor murder case. She died at age eighty-two, in August 1984. Of the three principals in the case—Taylor, Normand, Minter— all of whom wrote poetry, Mary wrote more poems and longer ones. Perhaps this example—its theme unrequited desire, something she fully understood—provides a fitting end to the story of her strange life. Though her real name was simply Juliet Reilly, she signed the poem "Mary Juliet O'Reilly":

> *Have you never been caught off your guard*
> *when you've heard*
> *Voices that called you with never*
> *a word?*
> *Or catching the scent of the forest*
> *pine-spiced,*
> *Sat yearning anew for a dream*
> *unsufficed?*
> *So wanton the wind on a still summer's*
> *night*
> *You forget you're forgotten and thrill with*
> *delight*
> *At the play of the cloud shadows high over*
> *the sea,*
> *Moon-lit to shimmering ecstasy. . . .*

Mary Miles Minter

The moon like a belle of old Spain hides
    her face
Neath star-sequined scarves of silver-tipped
    lace
As her radiance limns the clouds billowing
    black
And she laughs at your sorrow and shrugs
    at your lack.
Now parts she her veils and looks down
    from the skies:
"Poor mortal," she counsels, "love less and
    be wise."
And you answer, "Oh goddess of cold white
    fire,
Rejoice in thy godhead that knows not
    Desire."

9

The Inquest

THE CORONER'S inquest was convened at the Ivy Overholtzer mortuary at 10:00 a.m. on a rainy Saturday morning, February 4, 1922, three days after the murder. It was unusual in at least two respects: for brevity—it lasted less than an hour, as compared with the inquest for the Fatty Arbuckle case, which took seven hours—and for the fact that Coroner Frank A. Nance asked only five people to testify, when thirteen people had been served with subpoenas. Oddest of all was the fact that Faith MacLean, sitting in the room, was not put on the stand.

As soon as the fifth person to testify, Detective Sergeant Thomas H. Ziegler, had answered all the questions put to him, Coroner Nance suddenly said, "That is all the evidence we will take in this case. All but the jury will be excused." The uncalled witnesses and the many spectators in the crowded room, who had been expecting a detailed inquiry, were visibly puzzled. Among those receiving subpoenas who were not asked to testify were Faith and Douglas MacLean, E. C. Jessurun, Edna Purviance, Verne Dumas, Mrs. E. C. Reddick; Mabel's chauffeur, William Davis; and Julia Crawford Ivers. The coroner's failure to call Mrs. Ivers, who was closer to Taylor professionally than anyone else in Hollywood, meant that her unique contribution to the record has been lost.

Newspaper writers wondered why the coroner ended the inquest so abruptly. One reporter described it as "a scene out of the Keystone Kops" when several detectives, including Captain of Detectives David Adams, rushed out of the room, piled into their car, and sped off, tires screeching, "on the trail of a mysterious clue." It was as if their exit had been staged to demonstrate that the inquest was of minor importance. It appeared that forces were working to control events, under the expert guidance of Will Hays. Paramount did not allow Mary Miles Minter to attend; she was still in a state of hysteria. Charles Maigne, Taylor's fellow director at Paramount and his next-door neighbor, who had been one of the first on the scene after the murder, was not subpoenaed.

Because Mabel Normand, who was to testify first, was late, the coroner started the hearing with Charles Eyton, general manager of Famous Players–Lasky (Paramount) Corporation, who stated that Detective Ziegler was present when he arrived at the scene. It was Eyton who reported the fact that Douglas MacLean and his wife said they had heard a shot the previous night. When the coroner asked when the shot was heard, Eyton replied: "Mr. Mac-Lean told me it was about eight or a quarter after eight, and Mrs. MacLean thought it was a little later." The exact time of the murder was a crucially important detail, yet when Ziegler later testified, correctly, that it was "along about fifteen or perhaps ten minutes to eight" that Mrs. McLean heard the shot, Coroner Nance did not comment on, or even appear to notice, the discrepancy. When he could have called on Faith MacLean for her testimony, one wonders why he was satisfied with the conflicting evidence of Eyton and Ziegler. It was Ziegler also who described how the stranger came out of Taylor's house after the shot and "stood and looked at her," when Faith herself might have given a more detailed firsthand account to the public. Her description of the gunman, given privately to the district attorney, did not surface until 1954.

Charles Eyton was not asked about his going upstairs alone, though he did volunteer the information that "detective Ziegler and myself went up there and saw" an unused revolver in Taylor's dresser. Eyton revealed that it was *he* who took charge of examining the body:

"I told him [the deputy coroner] he had better turn the body over to make sure, and he put his hand under Mr. Taylor's body, and found a little—when he pulled his hand out, it had a little blood on his hand. Douglas asked him what that was, and he said it evidently had run down from his [Taylor's] mouth, but I noticed that there was no trail of blood—Mr. Taylor's head was in a pool of blood—there was no trail of blood running down."

C o r o n e r : "There was a pool of blood under his head?"

E y t o n : "Under his head, yes, a little pool of blood. *I* [italics added] immediately opened up Mr. Taylor's vest, and looked, and looked on the right-hand side, and there was no mark. *I* looked on the left-hand side and saw some blood, and then *I* told the Deputy Coroner that *I* thought that evidence enough to turn his body over to see what would happen. *I* sent for a pillow to put under Mr. Taylor's head, and *we* turned him over—the Deputy Coroner and myself—and *we* pulled his shirt and his vest up, and *we* found the bullet wound." In other words, Eyton the studio executive rather than Deputy Coroner Macdonald considered himself to be in charge and was not embarrassed to admit it.

Macdonald did not testify. His superior, Dr. A. F. Wagner, who performed the autopsy, gave a technical account of the course of the bullet: "The bullet entered six and a half inches below the [left] armpit, and in the posterior axillary line, and passed inward and upward, passing through the seventh interspace of the ribs, penetrating both lobes of the left lung, and emerging on the inner margin of the left lobe, then traversing the mediastinum, passed out of the chest on the right side of the middle line, posterior to the right collar bone, and entered the tissues of the neck; and I found the bullet just beneath the skin, four and a half inches to the left of the outer side of the right shoulder, and on a line drawn from the top of the shoulder to the lower junction of the right ear. The left pleural cavity contained considerable clotted blood. The vital, chest, and abdominal organs were free from disease. The cause of death was gunshot wound of the chest." The jurors had no questions for Dr. Wagner and he stepped down. "Mabel Normand," Coroner Nance called out.

A police officer forced a passage through the crowd, and close behind him came the star, followed by Nurse Julia Brew, her companion. Mabel was pale and ill at ease, and she looked as if she had steeled herself for the questioning. She wore a brown three-quarter-length wool coat, with white checks and wide white wool cuffs and collar. Her fedora hat was a wide-brimmed green velour.

She wore a black skirt and a white blouse with lace collar, a black belt, and white gloves, and she held a lavender silk handkerchief in her hand. She gave her name and address, but seemed unprepared for the obvious next question.

C O R O N E R : "What is your occupation?"

She hesitated for a minute, perhaps wondering whether to say "film actress" or "star," and then found the answer.

N O R M A N D : "Motion pictures."

C O R O N E R : "Miss Normand, were you acquainted with Mr. Taylor, the deceased in this case?"

N O R M A N D : "Yes."

C O R O N E R : "Did you see him on the evening before his death occurred?"

N O R M A N D : "Yes, I did."

C O R O N E R : "And where did you see him?"

N O R M A N D : "Will I tell you when I went in there and when I came out?"

C O R O N E R : "Did you see him at his home?"

N O R M A N D : "Oh, yes."

C O R O N E R : "And you were with him about how long on that occasion?"

N O R M A N D : "I got there about seven o'clock, and left at a quarter to eight."

C O R O N E R : "And when you left his place, did you leave him in the house, or outside?"

N O R M A N D : "No, he came to my car with me."

C O R O N E R : "Where was your car?"

N O R M A N D : "Right in front of the court."

C O R O N E R : "On Alvarado Street?"

N O R M A N D : "Yes, on the hill."

C O R O N E R : "He accompanied you to your car?"

N O R M A N D : "Yes."

C O R O N E R : "Was he still there when you drove away?"

N O R M A N D : "Yes, as my car turned around, I waved my hand at him. He was partly up the little stairs there." She raised her gloved hand toward the jurors, demonstrating how she waved to him.

C O R O N E R : "At the time you was [*sic*] in the house, was anybody else in the house?"

N O R M A N D : "Yes, Henry, his man."

C O R O N E R : "Henry Peavey?"

N O R M A N D : "Yes."

C O R O N E R : "Do you know whether Mr. Peavey left the house before you did or not?"

N O R M A N D : "Yes, he did, he left about, I should say, about fifteen or twenty minutes before I left, but stopped outside and spoke to my chauffeur; we came out later."

C O R O N E R : "No one else except Henry Peavey was there?"

N O R M A N D : "That was all." The coroner paused, apparently uncertain of his next question.

C O R O N E R : "What time was it you say you left him—drove away from his place?"

N O R M A N D : "I left him on the sidewalk about a quarter to eight."

C O R O N E R : "Did you expect to see him or hear from him later that evening?"

N O R M A N D : "Yes, he said—he had finished his dinner—he said would I go out and take dinner with him and I said no, I was tired; I had to go home and get up very early; he said he would call me up in about an hour."

C O R O N E R : "Did he call you?"

N O R M A N D : "No, I went to bed; if he called me I

was asleep; when I am asleep he tells my maid not to disturb me."

CORONER : "Was that the last time you saw him, when you left him about a quarter to eight?"

NORMAND : "That was the last time." There was a slight break in her voice as she said this. The jurors had no questions for her, and Mabel was excused.

Henry Peavey, the next witness, was the only person at the inquest who exhibited extreme outward signs of grief. When he was taken in to view Taylor's body before the hearing began, he had broken down and wept at the sight of his employer. On the stand he wore a yellow silk shirt and a dark bow tie. After testifying that he had worked as "cook and valet" for Taylor for "about six months," he said that on the night of the murder, when he left the house about a quarter past seven, Mabel Normand and his boss were seated near the dining room, and "they were discussing a red-backed book."

CORONER : "When you went out, which way did you go out, at the front or the back?"

PEAVEY : "I went out the front way. I always lock up the back door when I go out. I always lock the back door screen; it has a hook on the inside. I use the front door to come out all the time."

CORONER : "Did you carry the back door key with you?"

PEAVEY : "No, sir. I always turn it in the door and leave it just as it is."

CORONER : "Now, when did you next see Mr. Taylor?"

PEAVEY : "The next morning, when I went to work."

CORONER : "What time are you in the habit of coming to work?"

P E A V E Y : "I am usually there about half past seven."

C O R O N E R : "What time did you arrive there the next morning?"

P E A V E Y : "At just about half past seven."

C O R O N E R : "On arriving there, what did you do?"

P E A V E Y : "I picked up the paper [from the porch] first. I stopped in a drugstore on the corner of 5th and Los Angeles to get a bottle of medicine—milk of magnesia, he usually takes that every morning; I bought that on my way out. I picked up the paper and unlocked the door." He hesitated, and began breathing heavily. "The first thing I saw was his feet. I looked at his feet a few minutes and said, 'Mr. Taylor.' He never moved. I stepped a little further in the door, and seen his face, and turned and ran out and hollered."

At this point Peavey broke into sobs and could not go on. His loud sobbing and hooting sounded so much like laughter that it caused a few spectators involuntarily to smile. Then his sobs grew louder and more hysterical, and as he doubled forward in the chair, his shrieks caused a sensation. Several women spectators appeared to be frightened as he cried out brokenly, covering his face with his big hands. Finally, Peavey composed himself, drying his eyes with a colored silk handkerchief, and the questions resumed.

C O R O N E R : "Who did you summon? Who did you call to?"

P E A V E Y : "I don't know."

C O R O N E R : "You just made a lot of noise to attract all the attention you could?"

P E A V E Y : "Yes, sir." He described the various residents of the courtyard who responded, and the coroner reverted to the previous night's events.

CORONER: "You didn't come back there after you had gone away, when Miss Normand was there with Mr. Taylor?"

PEAVEY: "No, sir." He started crying again.

CORONER: "When you went out, was anybody around the place?"

PEAVEY: "Only Miss Normand's chauffeur; he had his lights all on inside the limousine, cleaning it. I hit him on the back and stopped and talked to him a few minutes."

The questioning returned to the next morning.

CORONER: "When you first opened the door, did you see any furniture overturned, or any sign of a disturbance in the house?"

PEAVEY: "Nothing more than a chair that was sitting next to the wall had been pushed out a little bit and his feet was under this chair."

CORONER: "And did you notice whether anything had been taken off of his body, or not—any jewelry?"

PEAVEY: "I didn't notice that. I didn't touch him at all."

CORONER: "Do you know whether he wore any valuable jewelry?"

PEAVEY: "Yes, sir, he had a wrist watch and another watch with a lot of little trinkets on; and a thing you stamp checks with to keep anybody from making the check any bigger, and a lead pencil."

CORONER: "Did he have a diamond ring?"

PEAVEY: "Yes, sir, he had a large diamond ring that he wore."

CORONER: "Do you know whether he had it on that evening?"

P E A V E Y : "Yes, sir, he was dressed just as when I went that evening, as I found him the next morning."

C O R O N E R : "Was the ring on his finger the next morning?"

P E A V E Y : "Yes, sir, his other jewelry that I had put away the night before was just as I had put it away up in the dresser drawer."

C O R O N E R : "You didn't find anything taken from the apartment?"

P E A V E Y : "No, sir, it was just as when I left it when I found it. The rug was a little bit kicked up. It looked like he had kicked it with his foot."

One of the jurors now asked Peavey whether any of the windows had been left open that night.

P E A V E Y : "No, sir, we had those little long pins that runs in the windows. The windows upstairs in his bedroom were up. The windows downstairs I always locked with this peg that slipped in the window."

C O R O N E R : "Were they still that way in the morning?"

P E A V E Y : "They were still that way in the morning. The lights were burning just as I had left them that night; two lights, one in the living room and one in the dining room."

The coroner excused Peavey from further questioning.

The final witness was Detective Sergeant Ziegler, who was asked what he found when he arrived on the scene.

Z I E G L E R : "I found the deceased, Mr. Taylor, lying just inside of the door, on his back. His hands, one of them, apparently to the side of his body, and the other lying outstretched; and blood pouring from his mouth. [The blood was already caked around his mouth rather than "pouring" from it.] He was lying with his head to the east, flat on his back, dead."

C O R O N E R : "Was his body rigid and cold?"

Z I E G L E R : "It was."

C O R O N E R : "Indicating he had been dead for some time?"

Z I E G L E R : "Yes, sir." He then described the neighbors who were present.

When the coroner asked about the reports of a gunshot the previous night, Ziegler gave the time accurately and corrected Eyton's account.

Z I E G L E R : "I learned . . . from Mrs. MacLean that along about fifteen or perhaps ten minutes to eight, the night before, she heard a shot. She thought it was a gunshot. She went to her front door and opened the door, and saw a man standing in Mr. Taylor's door. She looked at him, and he stood and looked at her; and he walked down the steps, turned to the left, and going around the end of the building, which is to the east; and out into the street."

C O R O N E R : "Did Mr. Jessurun tell you he heard a shot?"

Z I E G L E R : "I think he did."

C O R O N E R : "Did he say why he didn't try to investigate it?"

Z I E G L E R : "He did not. He didn't know but what it was an automobile making a noise."

C O R O N E R : "Did Mr. MacLean endeavor to investigate it?"

Z I E G L E R : "Not that I know of, and Mrs. MacLean's maid also heard a shot."

They discussed the unused revolver, a .32 automatic Savage, found in Taylor's dresser, and noted that the bullet found in Taylor's body was a .38 caliber.

At this point, the coroner said, "That is all the evidence we will take in this case. All but the jury will be excused."

The Inquest

The inquest had lasted a little over forty-five minutes. Faith and Douglas MacLean, Edna Purviance, Julia Crawford Ivers, other uncalled witnesses, and the crowd of spectators began to file out. Suddenly Captain of Detectives Adams rushed into the room and summoned Detective Sergeants Cline, King, and Ziegler, all of whom sped off in the police car to a destination unknown.

Mabel Normand's limousine had been backed into the alley behind Overholtzer's, and she now made haste to reach it. She was photographed at the back entrance, accompanied by District Attorney Thomas Lee Woolwine, who wore a formal suit and vest with a wing collar—the kind that soon disappeared completely in the postwar period—and Deputy District Attorney William C. Doran, who wore a business suit (see page 129).

About a week later Mabel accompanied Woolwine to Taylor's bungalow to rehearse for him her movements on the night of the murder. Step by step, she went over every detail of her visit with Bill Taylor on the fatal evening. Afterward she asked for permission to go upstairs to Taylor's bedroom. There she was photographed sitting in front of Taylor's dresser. She was looking for the packet of her letters to him, which she remembered he kept in the dresser. They were not there.

Mabel's concern about the letters seemed excessive, since she had explained that they were harmless exchanges between good friends, with no bearing on the murder case. Her stilted statement protested too much:

"These letters are all of such a nonsensical nature that they have absolutely no value, except as they exhibit and illustrate the good fellowship which existed between Mr. Taylor and myself. My letters were all so childish and

173

Rare photograph of Mabel Normand in Taylor's bedroom (his bedstead visible in mirror), accompanied by District Attorney Woolwine. She did not find her letters.

so simple that they could have meant nothing but perhaps a moment's cheer to so wonderful a man as Mr. Taylor. He was not like younger men, who always want me to put on evening clothes and go out somewhere to dance and dine. He liked to sit at home and talk about books." Yet it was learned that Taylor attended a dancing class for a lesson on the afternoon of the murder, perhaps to show that he could keep up with her younger beaux.

Mabel also said she would not mind if the whole world saw the letters, except that they might be misunderstood. Though at first the letters could be found nowhere in the house, after District Attorney Woolwine had made several thinly veiled threats about them they turned up, as if by magic, in the toe of one of Taylor's riding boots in his bedroom closet.

Detectives found them there, oddly enough, during a time when Charles Eyton happened to be in the house. He never acknowledged that he had returned the letters, though much later he admitted to having taken "a few things, to avoid scandal," on the morning of the discovery of the murder. Obviously, before the letters were brought back and deposited in the boot, Eyton had reviewed them carefully.

Woolwine, when he restored the packet to Mabel, called the letters "the usual vaporings of people in love." The samples quoted in the press were labeled the "Blessed Baby Letters." They were innocuous enough: "Dear Mabel: I know you're an awfully busy woman and haven't much time to grant to a poor duffer like me, but—how about dinner together next Wednesday and then the Orpheum. Yours always, Bill." "Dearest Desperate Desmond: Sorry I cannot dine with you tomorrow, because I have a previous engagement with a Hindoo Prince. Some other time. Blessed Baby."

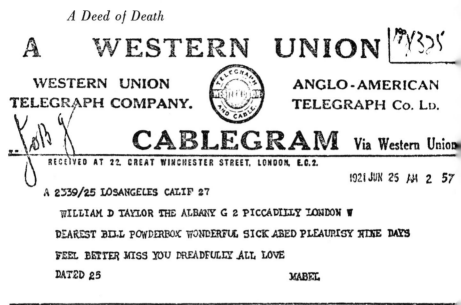

A WESTERN UNION

WESTERN UNION
TELEGRAPH COMPANY.

ANGLO-AMERICAN
TELEGRAPH Co. LD.

CABLEGRAM Via Western Union

RECEIVED AT 22, GREAT WINCHESTER STREET, LONDON, E.C.2.

1921 JUN 25 AM 2 57

A 2539/25 LOSANGELES CALIF 27

WILLIAM D TAYLOR THE ALBANY G 2 PICCADILLY LONDON W

DEAREST BILL POWDERBOX WONDERFUL SICK ABED PLEAURISY NINE DAYS

FEEL BETTER MISS YOU DREADFULLY ALL LOVE

DATED 25   MABEL

No inquiry respecting this Message can be attended to without the production of this paper.

Mabel Normand cables Taylor at Knoblock's London apartment in 1921.

There was a 1919 telegram, which Mabel sent to the Massachusetts location where *Anne of Green Gables* was shooting; it was playfully addressed to Captain W. D. Taylor, though he was no longer in the army. A cable she sent him on June 25, 1921, while Taylor was in London, staying at Knoblock's Albany flat, revealed that she was suffering from "pleaurisy": DEAREST BILL: POWDERBOX WONDERFUL. SICK ABED PLEAURISY NINE DAYS. FEEL BETTER. MISS YOU DREADFULLY. ALL LOVE. MABEL. There was nothing scandalous in the letters released, unless of course "pleurisy" was a code word for drugs. The real scandal, which Woolwine ignored, was that the letters had been removed from the scene of a murder and possibly tampered with.

176

The six members of the coroner's jury, all of whom were Los Angeles businessmen, had remained at Overholtzer's while Mabel left with Woolwine and Doran. The jurors quickly reached a verdict, expressed in an ancient formula. It was a printed form, with the blanks filled in by the coroner. (The parts handwritten by the coroner are indicated by italics.) The letter of the law, if not its spirit, was observed:

Verdict of the Coroner's Jury

State of California
County of Los Angeles } SS.

In the Matter of the Inquisition upon the body of *William Desmond Taylor*, Deceased, before Frank A. Nance, Coroner.

We, the Jurors summoned to appear before the Coroner of Los Angeles County *at Ivy H. Overholtzer's, Los Angeles, California,* on the *4th* day of *February, 1922,* to inquire into the cause of the death of *William Desmond Taylor,* having been duly sworn according to the law, and having made such inquisition after inspecting the body and hearing the testimony adduced, upon our oaths, each and all do say that we find that the deceased was named *William Desmond Taylor,* a male, married, a native of *Ireland,* aged about *45* years, and that he came to his death on the *1st* day of *February, 1922,* by *gunshot wound of the chest inflicted by some person or persons unknown to this jury with intent to kill or*

177

murder, and of which we duly certify by this inquisition in writing, by us signed this *4th* day of *February, 1922*:

EDWIN A. CLARK   Foreman:

JOHN R. WOODBRIDGE   E. JAY REID

R. J. STEIN

RIALTO F. C. LEITHOLD   FRANK A. NANCE

E. P. THOM   Coroner

10

Mabel's Story

O<small>N THE DAY</small> after the inquest, Edward Doherty, a leading reporter for the *Chicago Tribune*, wrote: "The [Taylor] murder may never be solved, say the police. Twenty people are said to be under suspicion. Twenty theories of the crime are being aired, but there has been not one arrest and not one clue. It is believed the movie interests would spend a million *not* to catch the murderer, to prevent the real truth from coming out."

The studios were alarmed by news reports like this and organized a press committee to "assist" reporters in covering the Taylor case. It was headed by Frank Woods of Paramount, a former newspaperman, a veteran scenarist, an early movie critic, and a former associate of D. W. Griffith. Each day, Woods reported to his superiors at the Hays office on the newspaper treatment of the case. "The newspaper correspondents," according to Terry Ramsaye, "became marked and observed men. They were run down, roped, hog-tied, taken to lunch (without cocktails), and regaled with filtered facts."*

Eddie Doherty and Wallace Smith, also from Chicago, were the two newsmen who stood out in resisting studio pressure. They learned it was considered a sacrilege to print anything detrimental to the movies. "Sacrilege and *bad business*," wrote Doherty, who said that he and Smith became "outcasts in Hollywood. . . . Ray Leek, who had invited us as honored guests to a Wampus [Paramount] dinner, called and cautioned us not to attend," because " 'the boys might cut your throats.' "

Undersheriff Eugene Biscailuz actually summoned Doherty and Smith to his office, in an attempt to intimidate them with the warning that they were in physical danger. Doherty hotly defended his responsibility to tell the truth as he saw it, and pointed out that the studios could sue him for libel if he did not tell the truth. The undersheriff replied: "That isn't the point. The industry has been hurt. Stars have been ruined. Stockholders have lost millions of dollars. A lot of people are out of jobs and incensed enough to take a shot at you." Officers of the law appeared more concerned about the movie industry and the sensibilities of the moguls than about solving the murder.

The studios seemed to be fearful that if certain aspects of the case were exposed, it would exacerbate their problems. In discussing the Taylor case in 1968, King Vidor said: "Last year I interviewed a Los Angeles police detective, now retired, who had been assigned to the case immediately after the murder. He told me, 'We were doing all right and then, before a week was out, we got the word to lay off.' "†

* Terry Ramsaye, *A Million and One Nights: A History of the Motion Picture*, 2 vols. (New York: Simon & Schuster, 1926), p. 819.

† King Vidor, letter to the author, November 12, 1968.

Eddie Doherty's story implied that "the movie bosses in power in Hollywood" controlled the police. He bluntly stated that studios meant "to prevent the real truth from coming out, to avert the exposure of Hollywood, and to squelch (before it is born) the scandal of the century." Almost all his references were to drugs:

> The movie bosses . . . feel the less said about Taylor the better. "They" fear the public may learn that Tillie Hopscotch, who played a sweet country girl in the latest Blah release, entertains her friends with orange juice and gin or beer and ether, or some other queer mixture with a kick. . . . Hop peddlers have become as rich as bootleggers here. Opium is needed after the nervous strain of the day. Jack Pickford's debauches in Paris cost him his wife. Marihuana makes Hollywood pulses leap. Hypodermic needles make stars sing beside the feathery palms and eucalyptus trees. Among these spoiled children William Desmond Taylor lived.*

Obviously Doherty suspected more than he could prove. He presented no hard evidence and, for fear of libel, mentioned no names except, as in the case of Jack Pickford and his wife, Olive Thomas, where the scandal had previously been covered in the press.

Doherty's fellow Chicagoan, Wallace Smith, took a bolder line and started a series on the drug aspects of the Taylor case. He was careful not to give Mabel Normand's name, but he identified her circumstantially. Almost from the start of her long career in the movies, Mabel's name had been associated with that of Mack Sennett.

---

* Edward Doherty, *Gall and Honey* (New York: Sheed & Ward, 1941), pp. 196–202.

Mabel Normand had turned twenty-nine three months before Taylor's murder, yet she was a veteran Hollywood star. She started in New York in 1909, appearing with John Bunny and Flora Finch in comedies produced at Vitagraph, weeks before Mary Pickford added to her stage earnings by moonlighting "in pictures" with D. W. Griffith at Biograph. Two years earlier, at age fifteen, Mabel had launched her career as an artist's model. A New Yorker, born on Staten Island in 1892, she was one of James Montgomery Flagg's favorite models. He admired her long black curly hair, large brown eyes, and slender, well-formed body, and his drawings made her a popular cover girl in magazines of the period.

It was after she left Vitagraph (in Brooklyn) for Biograph (in Manhattan) that she met Mack Sennett, who encouraged the studio to exploit her talents as a swimmer. Movies like *The Diving Girl, A Squaw's Love,* and *The Water Nymph* showed off her lovely figure in a form-fitting black woolen bathing suit. This costume, a sort of body leotard that left her arms bare, was made famous by Annette Kellerman, an earlier aquatic star on the stage and in Vitagraph films. When Sennett inaugurated the Keystone Comedies late in 1912, he took Mabel to Hollywood to be his leading actress.

With the immediate success of Keystone, Sennett was hailed, somewhat inaccurately, as the "father of American film comedy." James Agee has brilliantly described the special appeal of Sennett's movies: "Millions of people loved the Keystones' wild animal innocence and glorious vitality, their sincerity and sweetness," much of the latter being provided by Mabel.

Theodore Dreiser became so fascinated by Sennett's

inventiveness that he journeyed to Hollywood to interview him. The surreal qualities of Sennett's movies particularly appealed to the author of *Sister Carrie*: "The trains or streetcars or automobiles that collide with one another and by sheer impact transfer whole groups of passengers to new routes and new directions! Are not these nonsensicalities illustrations of the age-old formula that underlies humor? Isn't this an inordinate inflation of fantasy to heights where reason can only laughingly accept the mingling of the normal with the abnormal?"

Dreiser called Sennett "a creative force in the cinema world. Within his range, what a master—he is Rabelaisian!" Sennett was not an intellectual, but it would be foolish to suppose he did not know what he was doing. Mabel's series of comedies with Fatty Arbuckle, under Sennett's direction, made both actors internationally famous. Then came Charlie Chaplin.

Chaplin made his first films for Sennett in 1914. After a false start as a silly-ass English fop in *Making a Living*, he quickly found his real comic identity as the little tramp. Mabel directed three or four of the earliest Chaplins, in which she also appeared, but she and Sennett recognized that the English comedian had a special genius, and he was wisely allowed to proceed on his own. He made thirty-five one-reel comedies at Keystone during his first year, and would probably have made fifty-two, one each week, if Sennett had not starred him and Mabel with Marie Dressler in the feature-length *Tillie's Punctured Romance*. After Chaplin's one-year contract was up, he demanded a bigger raise than Sennett would agree to. The comedian left, to achieve further worldwide fame and an enormous fortune. This is Chaplin's opinion of the Mabel he knew and worked with at Keystone:

Two Mabel Normand portraits, one of which she has inscribed to her mother.

"Mabel Normand was extremely pretty, with large heavy-lidded eyes and full lips. . . . She was lighthearted and gay, a good fellow, kind and generous, and everyone adored her." His autobiography reveals that they almost became lovers. It happened in San Francisco, as they were getting ready to leave a late-night charity affair: "For a moment, we were alone. She looked radiantly beautiful, and as I placed her wrap over her shoulders, I kissed her and she kissed me back. . . . Later I tried to follow up the episode, but nothing came of it. 'No, Charlie,' she said good-humoredly, 'I'm not your type, neither are you mine.' " *

Mabel's type at that point was Mack Sennett. She depended on him completely; he had guided her career at every stage, arranged her contracts, advised her on roles, and made her the star of the Keystone lot. Mabel's psychological insecurity was all too obvious. Perhaps it arose from the fact that she had had little education aside from a few years at grammar school, and suddenly found herself a national celebrity. Sennett was equally uneducated, but he was self-confident and shrewd enough to get sound financial backing and remain the undisputed manager of his company in this period. Under his management, Keystone was a financial success from the start.

Everyone had expected Mack and Mabel to marry, including Mabel's parents and Mack's domineering Irish-Canadian mother, who had met the Normands in Staten Island during the Biograph days. The wedding date had even been set late in 1915. Why was it called off by Mabel early that summer? A new actress on the lot, Mae Busch, whom Mabel had persuaded Mack to hire, had become one of her close friends. At least Mabel thought so, until

* Chaplin, *My Autobiography*, p. 156.

someone warned her that "something was going on." Her
suspicions aroused, she burst into Mae's bedroom one
night in June and found Mack in bed with her. There was
a fight, and Mae hit Mabel with a heavy object. With blood
streaming down her face, Mabel staggered to the Ar-
buckles' house nearby and collapsed into their arms.
Fatty and Minta Arbuckle drove her to a private hospital,
where it took her several weeks to recuperate from the
concussion.

The papers carried a bowdlerized version of the story,
stating that Mabel had been injured on the set. In his
autobiography, Mack Sennett said: "The headlines were
two inches high. A sensationally written story, based on
no fact, said Mabel was dying. Actually she was staging
a thriller to get even. I was not allowed to see her. . . . She
lived for several weeks with [the Arbuckles]." * Mack,
who outlived Mabel by decades, maintained to his death
that he loved her and wanted to marry her, but for Mabel
that part of it was over.

Months after the incident, Mabel was interviewed in
Photoplay about the risky stunts she often performed in
films without using a stand-in. She answered one question
bitterly: "Why have I never been killed? Well, *I have
been*. Don't you read the Los Angeles papers?" She even
revealed her inner feelings about the crisis: "You know,
I never make plans. What's the use of making plans to go
places or marry people, when like as not you'll have to
write a note saying, 'Excuse me, I did want to become your
blushing bride today, but now it's no go.' "

Mack's betrayal was a trauma from which Mabel would
not easily recover. Everyone noticed how she changed in

* Mack Sennett, *King of Comedy*, as told to Cameron Shipp (Garden City, N.Y.: Doubleday & Company, 1954), pp. 198–9.

the months following the canceled wedding. The experience made her reexamine herself, as well as Mack. She started to take an interest in serious writers, attempting Freud and Nietzsche, and would carry books wherever she went. She hired a French-language tutor and acquired books in French by Pierre Louÿs, Anatole France, and François Coppé. She now realized that Mack Sennett was not as strong and reliable as he appeared. She had outgrown the carefree and lighthearted Mabel whom Charlie Chaplin described at Keystone.

The silent-film star Blanche Sweet described Mabel's behavior in this period: "After Mabel had her troubles with Sennett over Mae Busch, whom I never met, she would ride with me in my chauffeur-driven car. We wouldn't talk much, but she found relief in my sympathy and company. She was not physically ailing in any way that I could see, but she was deeply depressed." *

There was a problem on Mabel's mind, said Blanche, who defined it as "exploitation." The great success of her contemporaries Chaplin and Pickford helped Mabel to perceive that she was relatively underpaid. She had also been ill-used in some of his ventures by the man she considered her protector. By 1914, Mabel had attained a salary of $250 a week, a star's pay. (At Vitagraph in 1909, five dollars a day for ordinary players had been considered good pay.) In 1915, Chaplin said, Sennett paid him "more money than I had ever been offered in my life—$150 a week for the first three months and $175 for the remaining nine" at Keystone. After one year, his success was so enormous and the demand for his movies so great that Sennett proposed raising his salary to $500 a week, followed by annual raises after the second year.

* Interview with Blanche Sweet, February 3, 1969.

Chaplin asked for $1,000 a week, which Keystone refused, and in 1916 he signed with Essanay for $1,250 weekly, with a bonus of $10,000 for merely signing the contract.

In 1914, Mary Pickford had been getting $385 a week from Adolph Zukor. Her weekly salary rose to $1,000 in 1915, then before the year's end to $2,000, and to $4,000 by January 1916. Pickford was the highest-paid player in movies, until Mutual offered Chaplin $10,000 a week plus a bonus, bringing his total pay for that year to $670,000, more than three times Pickford's.

Mabel knew she was not a superstar like Mary and Charlie, but she had a devoted following, and her movies were doing extremely well at the box office, so well that *Photoplay* now called her the "Queen of Comedy." At this juncture she told Sennett she would leave if he did not pay her $500 a week. He not only agreed promptly but, desperate to win back her affection, told her he would set up her own production unit and company within Keystone, at which she capitulated. He erected a new studio for her away from the old lots at Edendale, with a large sign reading THE MABEL NORMAND FILM COMPANY.

She made only one film there, *Mickey*. It was her biggest public success, but a delayed one. The irony was that despite the film's genuine appeal at the box office, all she earned from it was her salary, because Sennett, by the time *Mickey* was almost completed, had lost control of Keystone as well as the unit that was hers in name only. Far from regaining Mabel's affection, Sennett provoked her alienation completely. *Mickey* was for him a professional and a personal disaster.

Keystone had become financially involved with the new Triangle Corporation, backed by the Aitken brothers,

A film frame from Mabel at the Wheel *(1914) shows her cycling with Charlie Chaplin at Keystone.* BELOW, *a shot from her Goldwyn film,* Sis Hopkins *(1919).*

through whose corporate manipulations Sennett was deprived of his autonomy. That was the end of Keystone and of the Mabel Normand Film Company. Sennett's claim that *Mickey* cost only $150,000 and grossed $18 million may be true, but neither he nor Mabel shared in the profits. Betty Fussell, in her excellent biography,* was the first to unravel all the financial shenanigans that attended the making of *Mickey*. By the time Mabel finished her work in the movie, which was directed by Richard Jones (who resorted to hiding a few reels until he was paid the $16,000 owed to him), she was aware that she had been more ill-used than ever before. In the spring of 1917, she left Sennett and signed a five-year contract with Samuel Goldwyn, who was personally attracted to her and was courting her assiduously.

At age six, when I first saw *Mickey* in our neighborhood theater in New Jersey, I loved it. I vividly remember the log cabin where Mickey grows up as a prospector's daughter in the gold-mining West; the horse race she wins disguised as a jockey; and the scene in which she dangles perilously from the edge of a roof. *Mickey* was one of the first films to have a theme song—not on a sound track, of course, but played on the movie house piano—and I can recall perfectly the words and music, which everyone in our neighborhood was singing:

> *Mickey, pretty Mickey,*
> *Can you blame anyone*
> *For falling in love with you?*

Seeing the film again recently, through the courtesy of the Film Library of the Museum of Modern Art, I was ap-

* Betty Harper Fussell, *Mabel* (New York and New Haven: Ticknor and Fields, 1982).

palled by its primitivism and its too obvious hokum. Yet its high spirits and rags-to-riches theme, when it was released following the hysteria of Armistice Day in 1918 (it didn't reach my neighborhood until early 1920), had a strong appeal throughout the country. Mabel had reached the height of her fame.

Samuel Goldwyn, having left Famous Players–Lasky, had just changed his name from Goldfish and formed his own company in association with Archie and Edgar Selwyn, borrowing the second syllable of their name. (King Vidor said the current gag was why didn't Sam use *their* first syllable and *his* second?) Early in 1917, he launched the Goldwyn Motion Picture Company with nationwide newspaper ads and billboards featuring the faces of his six "big name" actresses: Mabel Normand, the first to be engaged; two other movie stars, Mae Marsh and Madge Kennedy; an opera star, Mary Garden; and two stage stars, Jane Cowl and Maxine Elliott. The three movie stars were the better investment.

The experience he had filming Mary Garden in *Thaïs* he described as "among the most troubled of my history." The movie was an expensive flop, because Garden could not perceive that her famous interpretation of the role in opera would not work on film, especially silent film. Goldwyn said she bitterly protested the ending, in which Thaïs, now a saint, is seen "dying like an acrobat." She complained to Goldwyn, "Did you see the way they made me die? Imagine a saint dying like that!" Goldwyn, having had all he could take, told her, "You'd have a hard time proving to anyone that you're a saint." Cowl and Elliott, both great figures in the theater, were also ineffective on the screen.

Goldwyn claimed that Mabel's comedies saved him from backruptcy in one difficult period. Not one of her sixteen Goldwyn films was artistically successful, but obviously they provided what audiences wanted and expected from her. Soon after her switch to Goldwyn, the success that followed the delayed release of *Mickey* made her name a household word.

Under her new contract, Mabel was scheduled to begin at $1,000 a week, rising incrementally to $4,000 weekly by her fourth year, with a share of the profits in the fifth. She moved from Hollywood to New York, and her first films were made in Goldwyn's studios at Fort Lee, New Jersey. She sent Sennett a bitter wire before she left California: START WORK SEPTEMBER FIRST [1917]. COMPANY SAYS I DON'T LOOK WELL. MUST REST AND GO AWAY UNTIL THEN, SO I WON'T BE ABLE TO PEEP AT YOU EVER AGAIN. MABEL.

In New York, Mabel stayed with her actor friends Raymond and Zabelle Hitchcock in Great Neck, Long Island. Goldwyn's business manager, Abraham Lehr, said that Mabel was dissatisfied and quarreled with the studio about her new salary, refusing to begin work until they paid her more money. Goldwyn made frequent motoring trips out to Great Neck, where Mabel usually refused to see him, though once she took a snapshot of young Sam in his new runabout. It was clear to her friends, and no doubt to Mabel, that Sam's interest in her was more than professional. According to Hedda Hopper, he was smitten. Under these circumstances, Mabel soon won the contract dispute; her beginning salary was raised to $1,500 a week.

Goldwyn released fifteen Mabel Normand films between 1918 and 1920. Her sixteenth and last Goldwyn

film, *Head Over Heels*, was held back after her departure from his company in April 1921. It was released in April 1922, to take advantage of her notoriety in the William Desmond Taylor murder case. In other words, Mabel completed only three years of her original five-year contract before she and Goldwyn agreed to part company. They were the years of her greatest emotional and psychological stress, when she first met Bill Taylor and appealed to him for help with her drug addiction.

Sam Goldwyn has revealed somewhat guardedly what he thought of Mabel in his memoirs.* Mabel confided to one interviewer that she was curious to know what he would say about her. She had much to be concerned about, but he had only praise for her. Wartime shortages had had his firm headed for receivership, when the Armistice changed everything, and soon members of the du Pont family invested $7 million in his company. One day, while the receivership was threatening, Mabel handed Goldwyn an envelope containing $50,000 in Liberty bonds to help tide him over. "Those interested in the personality of Mabel Normand," Goldwyn wrote, "can receive no more illuminating introduction" to her generosity and her "response to any human appeal." He saw her give a thousand-dollar check to "a poor girl stricken with tuberculosis, with a dependent family," and said that Mabel "was likely to go out and buy a hundred dollar beaded bag for a stenographer in our organization." He contrasted Mabel, "a creature of impulse," with Mary Pickford, "a systematized human being."

* Samuel Goldwyn, *Behind the Screen* (New York: George H. Doran, 1923), pp. 112–13, 116–18.

OPPOSITE: *Mabel took this snapshot of Sam Goldwyn when he visited her in Great Neck, Long Island, in 1919.*

Mabel, carrying a book, photographed with Sam Goldwyn (LEFT) *and Charlie Chaplin* (RIGHT) *at the new Goldwyn studio in Culver City in 1919.*

When drug addict Olive Thomas died in Paris: "Never have I seen such a passion of pity as Mabel showed for the unfortunate girl, such a passion of indignation as she expressed against those she believed responsible for the tragedy. . . . To a nature like this, so alive with human sympathy and understanding, it is easy to forgive much." Goldwyn also wrote: "The screen does not absorb all of her amazing vitality. Eagerly she turns to people, books, gaiety, strange scenes. She does not want to miss one glint of 'this dome of many-colored glass.' . . . The thing that makes her beloved is that going-out-of-herself to others."

Mabel's sixteen films for Goldwyn—mostly five or six reels in length—were churned out regularly about every seven or eight weeks, to judge from the copyright dates. Seven were released in 1918: *Dodging a Million, The Floor Below, Joan of Plattsburg, The Venus Model, Back to the Woods, Peck's Bad Girl,* and *A Perfect 36*; six in 1919: *Sis Hopkins, The Pest, When Doctors Disagree, Upstairs, The Jinx,* and *Pinto*; two in 1920: *The Slim Princess* and *What Happened to Rosa*. The last, *Head Over Heels,* was delayed until 1922.

If some of Mabel's close friends knew about her drug addiction, none of them was aware of a secret and shattering event during 1918—the birth of her stillborn child. This well-concealed event, known only to Mabel, Sam Goldwyn, Mamie Owens, and Julia Brew, surfaced in 1974. After her graduation in 1918 as a nurse from St. Vincent's Hospital in Hollywood, Julia Brew was sent by her superiors to the house at Seventh and Ventura where Mabel was confined to bed. Julia had been told the case was confidential; she was to speak to no one about it. Mabel also swore Julia to secrecy, and she kept her promise for fifty-six years.

In 1974, when she was ninety, Julia for the first time met Stephen Normand, who visited her in Hollywood to learn about his great-aunt's past. The fact that Stephen's grandfather, Claude Normand, was Mabel's brother apparently convinced Julia that the grandnephew should be told the secret. When Stephen revealed the story after his return east, I advised him to write it all down. He gave his notes to Betty Fussell to use in her book, where the story first appeared.

That day in 1918, Julia said, Mamie Owens showed her to the bedroom where Mabel was in labor, moaning quietly. Julia helped with the delivery; the baby, a premature five-month-old boy, was born dead. Sam Goldwyn, the father, who was waiting outside, came in and kissed Mabel on the forehead. "I'm so terribly sorry, Mabel," he whispered. Julia said Mabel did not reply, and that he left the room "because Mabel did not want to see him." Crying and trembling, Julia told Stephen, "You don't know what I went through all those years with Mabel." Julia, who married in 1928, remained close to Mabel as her private nurse as long as she lived, and was at her bedside when Mabel died of tuberculosis in 1930.

Eddie Sutherland, the young Keystone actor who directed Mabel and married Louise Brooks, accused a worker at the Keystone lots, Hughie Faye (also known as "the Count"), of being the pusher who put Mabel "on the junk, [along with] Wallie Reid and Alma Rubens," both of whom died as the result of their addiction. But Julia Brew Benson, Mabel's constant companion during her last years, swore in a signed statement that barbiturates were the sole drugs Mabel used. She and Stephen Normand may have believed this, but we have contrary evidence from people who knew and loved Mabel and had no reason to lie—people like Norma Talmadge, Anita Loos, Hedda Hopper, Miriam Cooper, Sidney Sutherland, and Samuel Goldwyn. They have all attested to Mabel's addiction to hard drugs.

Sidney Sutherland, Mabel's first biographer (no relation to Eddie), wrote: "Truth makes it necessary to report that Mabel was the special object of Taylor's interest in this regard [drugs]. For some time her friends had tried desperately to rescue her from an addiction brought on by her yielding to the sinister influence about her. Wally Reid and other stars led the way." Julia's conviction that Mabel was not addicted recalls Jesse Lasky's experience with the round-the-clock doctor assigned to Wallace Reid. In a period when ignorance and naïveté prevailed about drug-taking, a 1919 Bureau of Narcotics report showed that the incidence of drug use was at an all-time high.

Anita Loos, who lived and worked in Hollywood as a scenarist from the D. W. Griffith days, has described the beginnings of the drug culture: "The underworld, quick to take advantage of any new field, very soon moved in on Hollywood and set up headquarters in a suburb called Vernon. Movie actors quickly deserted the Hollywood Hotel as a playground and ventured out to the Vernon Country Club. . . . Hanging around the Club bar were pushers of dope. They had an easy time converting those simple young drunks into drug addicts, and among their first victims were two stars of the first magnitude, Wallace Reid and Mabel Normand." Loos considered her a tragic figure. "One of the strangest manifestations of Mabel's cocaine addiction was a frenzy for writing letters. She would write to anybody . . . about nothing at all, addressing salesgirls whose names she didn't know as, for example, 'Saleslady in Stocking Department' . . . Mabel died young, as many dope addicts do. My brother Clifford was her doctor." *

In his recent biography of Sam Goldwyn, A. Scott Berg has recorded the producer's discovery of Mabel's addiction during their first tryst at a hotel in Saratoga:

> Goldfish waited at Pennsylvania Station for Mabel to arrive . . . no doubt braced for her canceling yet another rendezvous. This time she showed up, in what appeared to be a state of excitement. They scurried to make the train, met in the dining car for dinner, then went to Mabel's berth. In his hurried way, he began kissing her. Mabel . . . excused herself for a moment. When she returned, her ardent suitor had trouble even recognizing her. Mabel's entire mood had been altered; everything about her seemed speeded up. She appeared amorous toward him for the first time, but there was so much frenzy to her behavior that it was frightening. She looked at him with glazed eyes. Goldfish pulled back, retiring to his own berth. Mabel spent the entire weekend completely high on drugs, locked in her room most of the time." †

One afternoon in 1918, when Mabel was staying at the Ritz in New York, Hedda Hopper and Zabelle Hitchcock found her still asleep in a room full of dead flowers she did not seem to notice. "The stench was unbearable," Hopper wrote.‡ When they searched for "the white pow-

* Anita Loos, *A Girl Like I* (New York: Viking, 1966), p. 116.
† A. Scott Berg, *Goldwyn* (New York: Knopf, 1989), pp. 81–2.
‡ Hedda Hopper, *From Under My Hat* (New York: Doubleday, 1952), p. 108.

der [cocaine] we knew Mabel had been using," they found it, flushed it down the toilet, and left without waking Mabel.

On another occasion, Norma Talmadge, a devoted friend, accompanied Mabel and Mae Marsh on a visit to Miriam Cooper (Mrs. Raoul Walsh) in Hollywood. Mabel, looking tired and haggard, disappeared into the bathroom and emerged a changed woman. Cooper wrote that "she whirled around the room, dancing and singing. Then, with her back to the mirror on the bathroom door, she flicked up her skirt and whooped: 'My ass is open to the world.'"* Mabel had had her snort of cocaine.

Mabel's background and Catholic upbringing—her favorite Hollywood charity was the Little Sisters of the Poor—intensified her sense of guilt, especially after the premature birth of her stillborn baby, which may have been drug-related.

One of Mabel's poems, entitled "Short, Short Story," goes as follows:

> *I'm bad, bad, bad!*
> *If there was one sprig of poison-ivy*
> *In a field of four-leaf clovers,*
> *I'd pick it up.*
> *If it was raining carbolic acid,*
> *I'd be the dumbbell sponge.*

In *Photoplay*, August 1921, Adela Rogers St. Johns discussed Mabel's health problems after the actress had left Sam Goldwyn. The columnist could not mention drugs, which would have harmed Mabel's career, nor could she say that William Desmond Taylor late in 1919

* Miriam Cooper, *Dark Lady of the Silents*, with Bonnie Herndon (Indianapolis: Bobbs-Merrill, 1973), p. 181.

had put Mabel in the hospital for a drug cure. While she was at Goldwyn's studio, "Mabel's health sank steadily," St. Johns said, "and then the Goldwyn lot knew her no more. But in the rock-ribbed hills of a New England state [it was in fact New York], in a small village and in surroundings without comforts or indulgences of any kind, a girl was beginning her real fight for life. For six months Mabel 'rested.' With that smiling courage of hers, she took up the steady soul-grinding task of building up a wrecked nervous system, of recuperating a weak and neglected body."

As Sidney Sutherland wrote, "Taylor is known to have incurred the active hostility of narcotic peddlers who roamed Hollywood in profusion at that time." Mabel knew that Taylor, who was in love with her, was the one person determined to help her.

In February 1922, the Wallace Smith newspaper series on the case focused on an unnamed "actress not entirely outside the pale of suspicion in the Taylor mystery." He identified her by describing the Keystone Comedies and Mack Sennett, the man who made her famous: "She entered the world of films by the old-fashioned knockabout slapstick comedy route. She was made a star by a famous producer whose name is known today by the quantity and quality of female pulchritude he has exposed before the camera."

Smith said the actress was "a young woman, except for premature aging from her use of morphine. Her dealings with the drug peddlers have been a matter of Hollywood gossip for months." She was persuaded to take "the cure" and, really ill, went to a hospital. "Slowly she fought her way back," but "the insidious ring of dope peddlers . . .

don't easily give up their human prey." Smith himself saw the actress and the director at a party shortly before Taylor was killed:

"There was a weary droop to her once pert and vivacious gestures. She swayed a little, leaning on her escort's arm." An actor pointed at her and said, "She's full of the stuff again." Smith is referring to a New Year's Eve party a month prior to the murder.

According to Mabel's testimony to District Attorney Woolwine, she and Taylor quarreled on that occasion. "We went to a New Year's party at the Alexandria," she stated in Woolwine's office, "along with Wesley Ruggles and Pat Murphy and Renée and Tom Moore, and somebody got awfully drunk. Bill [Taylor] wanted me to leave the party and I wouldn't. And I didn't speak to him all the way home." Woolwine: "You got the pouts?" Mabel: "Yes, and I got a little nasty." As she explained it, the cause of the quarrel was merely Taylor's annoyance at her neglect of him.

"I would run away from him and pay attention to a lot of other people. Bill would say, 'You're not treating me very well. When are we going home?' I'd say, 'For God's sake why do you stand around with that trick dignity of yours? You make me sick.' And he'd say, 'I'm not trying to be dignified. Don't you know I love you?' I'd say, 'Good God, don't be so melodramatic!' And then I wouldn't talk to him."

The real source of provocation—drugs, the taboo word—is of course unmentioned. But Henry Peavey gave Woolwine further evidence that Mabel's explanation of the "quarrel" omitted the real cause. The morning after the party, Peavey found Taylor sitting at his desk, weeping. He was writing a letter to Mabel and told his chauf-

Mabel on location for Suzanna *(1922),*
which was being filmed by Mack Sennett
when Taylor was murdered. Mabel, in
sombrero, stands next to the horse. Mood
music was provided by the violinist and
pianist at left.

feur to deliver it to her in person. When Peavey handed the note to Howard Fellows, the chauffeur spoke about the previous night: "Mr. Taylor cried all the way home in the car." Fellows, driving his weeping boss and a silent, half-drugged Mabel back from the party, felt sorry that such a festive occasion as New Year's had ended so badly. Thus the year in which Taylor would meet his death had anything but a happy beginning.

Wallace Smith's reports were plainly sarcastic in their references to the Los Angeles police department. He said federal investigators were proceeding "on the assumption that the murderer, unhampered by the work of the [local] police—who originally had decided for some hours that Taylor had died of natural causes—easily made his way back east." He also exposed the police failure to fingerprint the contents of Taylor's room on the morning his murder was discovered. Two days later, when this crucial evidence was requested, Taylor's furniture was so smeared with new fingerprints, mainly those of detectives, that the evidence was useless. It's no wonder Wallace Smith and Eddie Doherty were blacklisted in Hollywood.

Deputy Sheriff Harvey Bell told Smith about Taylor's fight with a pusher, "a big fellow" (meaning someone high up in the drug ring, if not its leader), who used to deliver Mabel's "stuff" in person at her back door. One evening, Taylor had called on Mabel just after the pusher arrived at the rear entrance. "Mabel was torn between the two men," Bell said, "each demanding admission from opposite sides of the house." When she asked Taylor to wait while she spoke to a tradesman, she seemed so nervous that he became suspicious and rushed to the back in time to see the pusher handing her the "bindles" in exchange for greenbacks. Taylor gave the pusher a terrific beating and seized both the money and the drugs.

On February 23, Assistant United States Attorney
Thomas Green, in charge of narcotics prosecutions in
federal court in Los Angeles, held a press conference. He
told reporters that William Desmond Taylor had asked
for his legal help in fighting the pushers who were selling
narcotics to "a film star of the first magnitude," with
whom Taylor was in love.

Thus for the first time confirmation came from official federal sources of a drug connection in the Taylor
case. Even then, Mabel was never mentioned by name,
and ordinary readers got no clues to the statement's
significance.

"Taylor came to see me one day," Green said to reporters, "and told me that a group of peddlers were selling narcotics to many persons of his acquaintance, including a number of moving picture folk. One woman in
particular, a film star of the first magnitude, he told me,
was a confirmed addict and was being pressed in every
way to purchase more and more of the deadly drugs. Her
bill for drugs, Taylor said, was as high as $2,000 a
month." (Some newspapers misquoted this as $2,000 a
week.) It seems probable that the actress was paying
for blackmail as well as for drugs.

"He [Taylor] seemed particularly interested in this
woman," Green continued. "I presume he was in love with
her and, as I read between the lines, I judged he not only
wanted to wipe out the ring generally but to save the
actress from the clutches of the parasites. He told me that
this actress friend of his had been thought to be cured
of the drug habit. I think it was heroin. But later she had
lapsed into the toils of the drug and nothing could stop
her—love, influence, or money—excepting the elimina-

tion of the men who sold her the dope. According to Taylor, she wanted to be cured. She had confessed her habit to him shortly after meeting him, and asked him to do everything possible to save her."

Tom Green had assigned only two men to check the studios to make "every effort to wipe out the ring." He said they got nowhere, because "the addicts were as wary as the peddlers and used every strategy against us." He added that Taylor had had a fight with one drug pusher, "the leader of the drug ring," whom he punched in the jaw and kicked into the street near the actress's home.

Paramount executive Benjamin Hampton revealed in his book that another dope peddler "had been warned by Taylor to keep away from the studio and to refrain from selling narcotics to any actresses, and had been thrashed by Taylor for failing to heed the warning." *

Tom Green was a federal officer. It is significant that no local officials—neither the district attorney's office, the sheriff's office, nor the Los Angeles police department— ever mentioned Taylor's anti-drug fight, let alone Mabel's drug addiction, in connection with the Taylor murder case. When newspaper accounts hinted at a drug connection, they invariably smeared the late director by implying that it was Taylor himself who was involved in the sale of drugs to actresses.

Taylor had provided the ring with a serious reason to kill him by confiscating the costly drugs and depriving their seller of his payment. Theodore Kosloff, a Paramount actor and dancer, had a story he felt obliged to tell the police about an incident that occurred while he was working in *The Green Temptation*, Taylor's next-to-last film.

* Hampton, *A History of the Movies*, p. 286.

"Late in 1921, while this film was in the final days of shooting outdoors on location," Kosloff said, "while the crew was setting up a new scene, I was walking with Taylor, discussing what he wanted me to do in my role. Suddenly from behind a clump of bushes, a stranger sprang up and glared at us. Taylor reacted with a suddenness almost as surprising, leaping to one side and facing the stranger. For a brief minute, the unknown man and Taylor stood without speaking, looking each other straight in the eye. Then the stranger turned and walked away." Kosloff said Taylor offered no explanation of the incident and resumed his conversation where he had left off. After Taylor's death, Kosloff remembered the strange encounter as "threatening" and wondered whether it was related to the murder. In this encounter, the pusher he had beaten up may have been indicating to Taylor that, unless he laid off, his life was on the line.

Another piece of the drug puzzle surfaced in New York a week later. It was provided by Captain E. A. Salisbury, a well-known explorer and documentary filmmaker and a friend of Taylor's. Salisbury called a press conference at the Waldorf Hotel in New York, where he had come to arrange for the Metropolitan Museum to acquire a collection of art treasures he had brought back from Borneo. This former U.S. Army officer had a home in Hollywood, where he had been in January.

"Just five days before Taylor was killed [i.e., January 27, 1922]," he told newsmen, "I had a long chat with him and he told me of the activities of a local drug ring he was fighting. The truth is that Taylor sacrificed himself to save a popular movie star from sinking deeper and deeper into slavery from the use of narcotics." Taylor had known the actress several years. "She confessed soon

Rare shot of Taylor with Theodore Kosloff (LEFT), *star Betty Compson, and an unidentified actor dressed as a clown, during production of* The Green Temptation *(1922), released after the director's death.*

after they met that she was addicted to the drug habit and asked for his help in fighting it." He said Taylor had spent $50,000 over the years for her rehabilitation. After she told him she was cured, Taylor was convinced she really was, until recently, when it was evident that pushers had got her back on the drugs. "In my opinion, he was slain by someone whose enmity he incurred in his effort to cut off the drug supply of the actress," Salisbury said. "Bill Taylor threatened to make an example of the drug peddlers in Hollywood, but they got to him first."

Salisbury defended the reputation of his friend and said that his years of acquaintance with the director "enable me to say with conviction that Taylor was *not* a member of the fast set in Hollywood." As a maker of documentary and travel films, Salisbury was outside the Hollywood establishment. Unlike actors and other studio personnel, he could not be harmed by the scandal of the drug traffic in any way. He was free to speak, though Hollywood did not report his words: no Los Angeles paper carried his firsthand account.

Washington was the next city to be heard from—not surprisingly, in the light of Will Hays's White House connections. The hand of the Hays Office was discernible in the gratuitous and irrelevant defense of the film colony inserted into the Washington press release. Ralph Oyler, director of the new Federal Narcotics Division, issued this awkwardly worded statement on drugs and the Taylor murder case:

> We have under surveillance on the Pacific coast some of the biggest drug vendors in the world, who are engaged in a concerted effort to corrupt and enslave to drug use motion picture people and others

of large earnings that they, the crooks, may profit by
levying tribute. This ring connects with one in New
York, one in Philadelphia, one in Canada, and with
smugglers who bring drugs from abroad—the greatest source of supply. . . . We have positive evidence
of the shipment of narcotics in truck loads from New
York to Los Angeles for sale there. One of these
trucks contained 250,000 heroin tablets. Another
truck, seized at Grand Central station in New York
and bound for Los Angeles, was checked out on the
ticket of Sam Levine, a recorded criminal, and contained opium and morphine.

*I want right now to remove all aspersions that
have been made against prominent motion picture
people. They are not guilty* [italics added]. In the
motion picture cities there are a few wealthy addicts,
and that is true of nearly every other community.
We find that the motion picture people as a class
marry, have children, and lead decent lives. Los
Angeles is not worse than any other city, our men
report. . . . I have men working on these cases, which
include the Taylor murder in Hollywood and recent
cases in New York.

Our findings would tend to show that the cases are
all connected and have their beginning in a criminal element, *directed by one master-mind, already
named in the newspapers* [italics added]. We are
not mentioning this criminal, and will not until we
have evidence sufficient to convict.

The "master-mind" Ralph Oyler referred to was "Dapper Don" Collins, one of the most stylish criminals of the
era. His colorful crimes and sophisticated methods fasci-

nated reporters and readers alike. He is said to have been the first blackmailer to wiretap telephone conversations; his other enterprises included bootlegging, robbery, the confidence game, and narcotics. His life could have furnished the scenario of a movie of the period. The eldest son of a New Orleans family, he gained a reputation in his youth as a racing bicyclist. Hired by a circus to ride a bicycle in a cage with two lions, he made national headlines by retaliating against his employer's financial injustice by opening the cage and releasing the lions. Attendance at the circus increased greatly.

Collins became a big shot in crime in 1921, when customs officials seized his ship, the *Nomad*, a converted U.S. submarine chaser, which he had sailed from the West Indies to the port of Camden, New Jersey, with a large cargo of contraband whiskey. (Collins acquired the ship by representing himself as Charles A. Cromwell, a millionaire.) In the Prohibition era, he headed his own criminal organization of two hundred confederates in large cities. His appearance and manners were gentlemanly, and he had friends in all walks of life. Having eluded the police successfully, he was spotted in Paris by an American detective seeking someone else and arrested on false-passport charges. In the sun-deck suite Collins was assigned on the French liner that brought him home, he held a press conference for New York reporters. He wore an oxford-gray suit, a fawn-colored topcoat and fedora, and polished shoes with spats.

When a reporter asked, "Don, are you broke?" he replied, "I'm never broke." He retorted to one reporter's "You are charged with many crimes" by saying, "Quite so, but I assure you I was not connected with the murder of the Czar of Russia. They charge me with everything, down to stealing doormats and milk bottles." This was in 1919, and soon he was free again. His life of crime caught up with him in 1939, when he was sentenced to fifteen years for extortion. He died in Attica Prison in New York State after eleven years behind bars.

It seems odd that the Federal Narcotics Division should have identified and publicized a connection between this Raffles-like figure and the drug aspects of the Taylor case. The New York police department revealed that "Dapper Don" Collins was in Los Angeles around the time of Taylor's murder. They had information that early in 1922 in Hollywood, he tried "to use a movie actress in a blackmail attempt." It seems hardly possible that he was the "big fellow" Taylor beat up at Mabel's back door, but who knows? Nor could Collins be the rough-looking young man Faith MacLean saw in Alvarado Court; a "mastermind" would have left such a chore to an underling. Why should Washington have characterized this international criminal as a "master-mind" and hinted at a connection with the Taylor murder case, "without sufficient evidence"? It is another mystery created by the law enforcement officials involved in the case.

Early in 1989 I applied to the Attorney General and to the Bureau of Narcotics, under the Freedom of Information Act, for access to the Ralph Oyler files on the Taylor murder case. Oyler's statement to the press admitted that "I have men working" on this case. The Department of Justice replied to me: "This office [the Freedom of Information Unit] has nothing to provide."

Mary Pickford's recollections of Mabel Normand were much warmer and more detailed than her comments on William Desmond Taylor. During the long telephone call

we put through from King Vidor's apartment in Hollywood in 1967, she said to me, speaking (to my surprise)
with a slight brogue: "I knew Mabel from the Biograph
days. We were good friends from the start, though I
couldn't see what she saw in Mack Sennett. There were
so many good-looking young actors around, but she was
partial to Sennett. He was something of a roughneck,
smoked smelly cigars, and chewed tobacco. Of course, I
was a Belasco actress before I went into the movies. Mabel
had no stage experience; she'd been an artist's model.
She was so pretty, with dark curls and dark eyes. I returned to the stage while still at Biograph, and Mr. Griffith bought the first two rows for the whole company on
opening night. Here I am lying in bed"—she was talking
from her home, Pickfair—"and I still smell the odor of
women's perfume that wafted over the footlights as the
curtain went up."

Did Mabel go with them to Hollywood when Biograph
first moved to the Coast? "Not the first year. We only came
out in the winter, when we needed the California sunlight
for photography. I think Mabel came with us the second
year, but in 1912 Mack Sennett started Keystone and
made Mabel their star."

Did she know about Mabel's drug addiction? "Absolutely not!" she replied, shocked by such a suggestion. "I
know there was talk about that, but I'm sure it's untrue. Mabel had consumption, you know, and that's what
she died of, but drugs . . ." Her voice trailed off in
disapproval.

What did Miss Pickford think of William Desmond
Taylor? "He was a perfect gentleman," she said. "When
he directed three of my movies, before he went overseas
with the Canadian Army, he did a really professional job.

He was very well read, you know, and quite English. My brother Jack and sister Lottie also made movies with him, and thought highly of him."

Did she think his murder was drug related? "Why, no! I never heard that. Wasn't it that servant he employed, the one who stole money and forged checks?" Efforts to keep her talking about the Taylor case were unsuccessful. "You know, when Mabel made a comeback in 1926, at the Hal Roach studios, I felt so bad about the career trouble she'd had, and the mistake she made in trying to adapt to the stage so late in her career. She was in a play that was tried out of town and never opened in New York, and the reviews said she could not project her voice. She took voice lessons with Nazimova, but Mabel never had to talk in movies, and it didn't work. She was a silent-film comedienne and one of the best."

Mary Pickford made a generous public tribute to her colleague in an ad in *Motion Picture World* on March 24, 1926:

> WELCOME BACK TO THE SCREEN, MABEL NORMAND
> Your return makes us all happy for you have the gifts, the training, the personality, and the technique which is the supreme technique—the one which is so sure it does not show. You have the rare thing, the possession above price, Mabel Normand, the charm of spontaneity! The best o' luck, Mabel, and welcome back to the screen.   MARY PICKFORD

Miss Pickford said she and Mabel shared a liking for things Irish, since their mothers were of Irish descent. "When I made *The Taming of the Shrew* with Douglas, you know, after sound came in, I sometimes slipped into an Irish brogue without realizing it. When they played the sound back, there it was. The rhythm of Shakespeare's blank verse brought out my brogue; we had to do retakes." It was an effort to refrain from mentioning her film's immortal credit line: "By William Shakespeare, with additional dialogue by Sam Taylor."

In the years following the Taylor case, Mabel Normand's life continued to be dogged by scandal and trouble. At a New Year's Day party at playboy Courtland Dines's house on January 1, 1924, her new chauffeur, Joe Kelly, used Mabel's gun to shoot Dines. Mabel had gone to the party with Edna Purviance, who was dating Dines. "We three were just the best pals in the world," Edna explained to the police, but it was Mabel whose name made the headlines.

Apparently Joe Kelly felt protective of Mabel. When he was summoned to the party by phone, the housekeeper, who took the obviously drunken phone call, had said to Kelly, "Mabel would be better off without such friends." Kelly told Inspector Cline (the former sergeant) that when he arrived, he found Mabel lying on a divan, "in no condition to stay there any longer." He begged her to let him take her home. Dines sneered at the chauffeur and, according to Kelly, reached for a bottle with which to hit him. "That was where the trouble came in," Kelly explained, and Cline asked what he meant by trouble. "I just shot him, that's all," said Kelly.

He claimed Dines kept Mabel "all hopped up." Did he mean with liquor or dope? Cline asked. "Liquor, I guess." "Is Miss Normand using dope now?" the inspector asked. "Not that I know of," said Kelly. Dines charged that Joe Kelly was a cocaine addict. The police in fact learned he was an ex-convict, whose real name was Horace Greer.

Mabel and her best friend, Edna Purviance, performing high jinks on Courtland Dines's yacht in 1923, before the shooting scandal broke.

He had shot Dines three times, wounding him only slightly; the jury decided it was in self-defense. Mabel, who felt that in this incident she was guilty in no way whatever, suffered a very bad press. The photo showing her, Edna Purviance, and Courtland Dines and their drunken larking aboard a yacht, which was plastered in all the papers, did not help Mabel's reputation.

In the aftermath of the Dines shooting, the states of Kansas and Ohio banned Mabel's films from their screens. "This film star has been entirely too closely connected with shooting affairs," the Ohio attorney general announced. But Mabel always maintained that "No ban ever was placed on any of my pictures because of the Taylor murder and the Dines shooting." She claimed that in both affairs, "I was promptly held guiltless and nowise responsible." She meant that the Hays Office never officially banned her movies, but resistance and boycott did occur regionally.

Mack Sennett sent her on a public relations tour, after the Illinois Federation of Women's Clubs and the Women's Association of Commerce joined in inviting her to present her side of the story. She arrived in Chicago, only to have Mrs. George Palmer, president of the Women's Clubs, publicly announce: "The majority of Illinois club women wish to see neither the actress in person nor on the screen." Mabel returned to Hollywood in humiliation.

Even the fan magazines betrayed her. One feature story, maliciously captioned "The Inside Dope on Movie Stars," described her in cruel words: "Her eyes are bulging and they have lost their old luster. Her voice is dull and, at times, wandering. . . . The old Mabel Normand of the serio-comic smile and quick wit is gone." In September 1924, she was named as co-respondent in Mrs. Georgia W. Church's divorce suit against her husband. Though two other women were also cited, only Mabel's name made the headlines.

Mabel had been a patient in Good Samaritan Hospital at the same time as Mr. Church. His wife claimed "the said Mabel Normand was then accustomed to run in and out of his room attired, as to her outer garments, only in nightgown and to have drinks with him there. . . . She kissed him goodbye on his departure from the hospital." Mabel was outraged. She told reporters she had never left her bed during her two-week stay in the hospital, and had waved the anonymous next-door patient a cheery goodbye when he was wheeled past her door on his way home. "Cross my heart, boys," Mabel said, "I wouldn't know the man if he were sitting here right now." She was so incensed she decided to sue for libel, against the advice of Mack Sennett and other friends. "There is a limit to all human endurance and I have reached mine," she said. She asked for $500,000 in damages to her name and reputation. She lost the suit. The state superior court ruled against her on technical grounds, holding that Mrs. Church had made no direct charges against Mabel Normand herself, but rather against Mr. Church.

The Nickel Hopper, released late in 1926, was one of the last five comedies she made for Hal Roach. In the movie, still shown occasionally at the Museum of Modern Art in New York, Mabel is a nickel-a-dance girl whose feet are stepped on by a young Boris Karloff, who towers over her, and by a fat young Oliver Hardy. When she spurns the hero's Rolls-Royce and gets into her own Ford "Tin Lizzie," it collapses around her in a heap, as in the well-known Laurel and Hardy comedies later produced by Hal Roach.

In September 1926, she suddenly married actor Lew Cody, a man-about-town and a boyhood friend of hers from Staten Island, also of French-Canadian ancestry, whose real name was Louis Coty. She had asked him to fill in at the last moment for a canceled guest at a convivial dinner party at her house. Around midnight, he fell on his knees and made a burlesque marriage proposal, which Mabel accepted in the same spirit. When the other guests demanded they elope, Cody called the Beverly Hills police station for a motorcycle escort. The wedding party took off in Mabel's car to Ventura, where they roused up a justice of the peace. After the wedding, Lew went to his club and Mabel went home; they never lived together, though as good friends they continued to go out together. On her death, Lew Cody renounced all legal claims on her estate.

In August 1929, Mabel was taken to Pottenger's Hospital with tuberculosis, and the faithful Julia Benson took a room nearby to attend to her. Mrs. Mary Normand soon arrived from Staten Island, but Mabel sent her mother home after a short visit. In January 1930, she received a card inscribed, "To Mabel Norman [*sic*]—Hope you recover soon, Samuel Goldwyn." There was nothing from Mack Sennett; he said that after she became "Mrs. Lew Cody, I never saw her or spoke to her again."

When Mabel's father died, on February 2, she was too ill to be told. Her older sister Gladys, an aviatrix, sent Julia the black-edged card announcing Claude Normand's death, with this note: "Julie darling, whatever happens please don't allow Baby to see this—at least we can spare her this." On February 22, Julia decided to send for a priest, and she wrote Stephen Normand, "He anointed MN, also the nuns from Mount St. Mary's came and brought holy water, the blessed candle, etc." Early on the morning of February 23, 1930, at 2:25 a.m., Mabel died in Julia's arms.

11

Impersonal Executioner

THE FRENCH WRITER Georges Simenon is famous for his series of crime novels in which the incomparable Inspector Maigret always unmasks the murderer. In *La Tête d'un Homme*, which Simenon published in 1940, the man whom Maigret knows (without proof) to be the murderer tries to bait him by bringing up the William Desmond Taylor case:

"Do you remember the Taylor case?" he asked Maigret abruptly. "I don't suppose you do, because you probably don't read American papers. Well, Desmond Taylor, one of the best-known Hollywood movie directors, was murdered in 1922. At least a dozen people's names were mentioned in connection with the case—stars, beautiful women, and so on. But no arrest was ever made.

"The case faded out. But there was an article about it not long ago in an American magazine. Do you know what it said? I have an exact memory: 'From the very beginning the police knew perfectly well who killed Desmond Taylor. But they had so little evidence that, even if the murderer had given himself up, he would have had to undertake the prosecution himself. He would have had to furnish the evidence that would corroborate his confession.' That's a year ago now. I remember every word of it. And of course Taylor's murderer is still in the best of health."

If the murderer was in his early twenties when he committed the crime, he would (if alive) be ninety or so today. The question remains whether enough evidence has survived to solve a murder that took place almost seventy years ago. The answer is that it should be possible, provided all the available facts are analyzed objectively. The chief mystery is: Why did the case go unsolved when a witness saw the murderer leaving the scene of the crime? The answer appears to be that those in power and in a position to exercise control preferred that the case not be solved. It is essential to summarize the known facts—not as given by the inept or powerless police at the scene but as sifted from the available evidence:

On the day of the murder, four men and two women saw the gunman. Another woman heard him in the alley prior to the murder, though she did not see him. The six described him as stocky ("between 165 and 175 pounds"), young ("about twenty-six or twenty-seven"), "rough-looking," around five feet seven, and wearing a jacket but not a raincoat or topcoat. He also wore a "light-colored" or "gray plaid" cap (and perhaps a scarf). The descriptions tallied enough to confirm that they all saw the same person. Murders have been solved with less evidence than this. These are the witnesses:

1 and 2   F l o y d   H a r t l e y   and his assistant, L . A . G r a n t . They told reporters that sometime around 6 p.m. on February 1, 1922, a strange man walked into their premises at the Hartley Service Station on the corner of Sixth and South Alvarado streets. They both said the man was twenty-six or twenty-seven, weighing around 165 pounds, with dark hair. He was wearing a dark suit—blue serge, they thought. When he asked where the residence of William Desmond Taylor was located, they pointed out nearby Alvarado Court. The police did not interview them.

3   M r s . M . S . S t o n e . She was baby-sitting for her daughter at apartment 412-A, Alvarado Court, opposite to and down from Taylor's bungalow. She told reporters that after 6 p.m. on February 1, she was on her way to her daughter's house, when she saw a stranger standing at the corner, apparently waiting for a streetcar. When he failed to board the next car, she wondered why he was waiting there and became a bit frightened. She waited at the lighted corner before crossing the street, and watched the man as he turned on Alvarado into Maryland, walking toward the rear of Taylor's bungalow. She saw him pause in front of the Hotel Alvarado and transfer some object from his left hip pocket to his right-hand jacket pocket. She proceeded to her daughter's house. Later—it was nearly 8 p.m., when she was taking her granddaughter upstairs to bed—she heard what sounded like a pistol shot. Not wanting to alarm the child, she put her to bed quietly and then looked down into the courtyard. She saw nothing, except "a weird pattern of light

and shadows." Her description of the stranger confirmed that he was "thinner than Sands," Taylor's fat servant, whom she knew by sight. The police did not interview Mrs. Stone.

4 C H R I S T I N E J E W E T T, the MacLeans' maid. She heard a man "walking in the alley" around 7:15 p.m. between the MacLeans' house and Taylor's. "I heard his shoes scrape on the pavement. At intervals he would move and stand still." It was Christine who insisted that the report she heard around 8 p.m. was a gunshot. Only because of her insistence, Mrs. MacLean went outside and looked over at Taylor's doorway. Christine never saw the person she heard, but her testimony is significant: women's shoes make a different sound on pavement than men's. Detective Ziegler questioned her at the scene.

5 and 6 E . W . D A S C O M B, streetcar conductor, and R . S . W O O D A R D, motorman. They saw a man board their inbound trolley at Alvarado and Maryland. They told reporters they both remembered him because of the infrequency of trolley stops at that point and also because their car was almost empty. Having had no reason to look at their watches, they guessed the stop was at either 7:54 p.m. or 8:27 p.m., because "those were the times on their schedule." As all travelers know, schedules can be elastic; the 7:54 might have been late or the 8:27 early. Faith MacLean said the man left Alvarado Court shortly after 8 p.m. Since an almost empty trolley could have meant fewer stops, the stranger may have boarded before 8:27. Dascomb and Woodard described him as "about five feet ten inches tall, around 165 pounds, about twenty-seven or so, wearing a hat or cap of a light color and also something tan, either his jacket or vest."

They mentioned no scarf. To their eyes, he seemed "fairly well dressed." The police did not interview them.

7 F A I T H M A C L E A N , the only eyewitness after the shot was fired. She was not asked to give evidence at the inquest. She listened to Charles Eyton's account of what she alone saw, and Eyton got the times wrong. The failure of the coroner, seeking the cause of death, to ask for her firsthand account is baffling.

When she heard the gunshot, just before 8 p.m., Mrs. MacLean went to the door of her house, which was at a right angle to Taylor's. A strange man emerging from Taylor's doorway looked straight at her—and stopped. Then he coolly went back, as if he'd forgotten something, quickly came out again, looking at Mrs. MacLean, who stood only a few yards away, and walked through the alleyway to Maryland. His calm behavior convinced Faith MacLean she was mistaken about the gunshot. Beyond doubt, this man was the murderer of Taylor. Let us call him Mr. X.

Faith said Mr. X was about five feet nine and wore a dark suit but not a topcoat. She also thought he wore a "gray, perhaps a plaid cap." She was not sure whether he had a scarf around his neck or if his jacket collar was turned up; it was either one or the other on this chilly night. She also said, "He was not a well-dressed man. He was dressed like my idea of a motion picture burglar." This was the sole discrepancy in the various descriptions of the witnesses, but whether Mr. X was "well" or "badly" dressed is a subjective matter.

Her description included nothing but masculine characteristics, like "a roughly dressed man." When the sheriff later suggested to her it might have been a woman dressed as a man, she said vaguely: "Well . . . I suppose it *might* have been." This is a crucial point. Hartley and Grant described a man walking into their gas station, Mrs. Stone saw a man transferring an object from his pants to his coat pocket, Christine Jewett heard a man's shoes scrape the pavement, Dascomb and Woodard had no doubt it was a man who boarded their trolley, and Faith MacLean's first account of the gunman looking straight at her left no doubt about the sex of Mr. X. Faith's later hesitant assent to the sheriff's theory sounds like an unconvinced and polite response to an official. In view of the overall testimony as originally given, it is reasonable to conclude that he was a man.

Christine Jewett placed him at the scene at 7:15 p.m., at a time when Mabel Normand was talking to Taylor in his rooms and Peavey was getting ready to leave. From the evidence of the cigarette butts, Mr. X was waiting outside in the alley, smoking steadily. This is the timetable of the events that night:

P.M.

6:00 —Mr. X talks to Hartley and Grant.

6:10 —Mrs. Stone sees him turning onto Maryland.

7:00 —Mabel arrives at Taylor's.

7:15 —Christine Jewett hears man in alleyway.

7:20 —Peavey leaves.

7:40 —Taylor escorts Mabel to her car.

7:45 —Mabel drives away.

7:58 —Gunshot heard by MacLeans et al.

8:02 —Faith sees Mr. X.

8:04 —Mr. X leaves by alley and boards trolley.

8:15 —Howard Fellows rings Taylor's bell.

A.M.

12:00+—Purviance sees lights on in Taylor's rooms.

7:30 —Peavey discovers the body.

When Taylor escorted Mabel to the car, leaving his door open or unlocked, Mr. X had ample opportunity to slip into the house. Judging by the upward trajectory of the fatal bullet, he shot Taylor from a low and probably crouched position. Perhaps he was hiding behind the living room door, awaiting Taylor's return. According to the coroner, "The bullet entered six and a half inches below the [left] arm-pit" and "entered the tissues of the neck," ending up "on the outer side of [Taylor's] right shoulder." This odd angle indicates it was the work of an experienced and extremely accurate gunman, who fired at close range. How close? When the coroner asked Detective Ziegler, "Did you investigate to see whether the clothing was powder-burnt or not?" he replied, "I did not."

Did Mr. X straighten out Taylor's body and clothes? We do not know. The director's tall figure may have fallen exactly as it was found. Since robbery was clearly not the motive, why should Mr. X have touched the corpse? His sole remaining problem was to get away safely, and he succeeded.

In the light of these facts, let us review the ten suspects whose names turned up during the investigation:

1 MRS. CHARLOTTE SHELBY. Old-time Hollywoodites like Adela Rogers St. Johns and King Vidor believed that the mother of Mary Miles Minter went to Taylor's house in men's clothes and shot him. It does make for a great movie scene, too melodramatic to resist. But St. Johns, who was in New York at the time of the murder, and Vidor, who was snowbound on location in the nearby mountains, merely read the newspapers, like everyone else. Diminutive Mrs. Shelby was almost fifty,

and the murderer was a rough-looking young man of twenty-six or twenty-seven. Betty Harper Fussell has pointed out that to match the descriptions of the witnesses, "Mother Shelby would have had to strap on elevator shoes six to eight inches high, and strap sixty to seventy pounds of padding to her body."* One hesitates to eliminate such a popular and well-qualified suspect, a monster of a woman hated by both her daughters, but facts are facts.

2 J U L I A C R A W F O R D I V E R S . The "little woman dressed in blue" was fifty-five in 1922. It would have been just as impossible for her to impersonate the youthful killer as for Mrs. Shelby.

3 M A R Y M I L E S M I N T E R . Young enough, but otherwise unqualified to impersonate Mr. X.

4 M A B E L N O R M A N D . Not eligible, since Taylor was killed immediately after she drove off.

5 M s . X . The police never used this identification, but they speculated about an unknown "jealous woman." If there was such a person other than those named, the witnesses' description of Mr. X eliminates a Ms. X.

6 E D W A R D S A N D S . The right age, and a suspicious character with a criminal record. But as Edward Knoblock surmised, having got safely away with Taylor's money, jewelry, and clothes, why would Sands jeopardize his safety by returning? Or if he did return, it made no sense for him to leave so much loot behind—diamond ring, money, etc. Mrs. MacLean and Mrs. Stone, who knew Sands, categorically denied he was the man they saw.

* Fussell, *Mabel*, p. 168.

7 DENIS DEANE-TANNER. The police, knowing it to be untrue, allowed the rumor to circulate that Denis was Sands. Forty-five, lean, and sandy-haired, Denis does not fit the description of the youthful, dark-haired Mr. X. Denis had no known motive to kill his brother.

8 HENRY PEAVEY. Peavey was taller and much heavier than Mr. X, and Faith MacLean saw a white man. Despite Florabel Muir's suspicions, Peavey was exonerated by the police.

9 MACK SENNETT. He acknowledged that (1) he was in love with Mabel and (2) he did not like Taylor. But he was forty-two, tall and heavyset, unlike Mr. X. After being questioned by the police, he was also exonerated.

10 MR. X. This man, seen by six witnesses, is certainly the murderer. Amazingly, the police never circulated his description, as they did that of Sands. Nor did they ever list Mr. X as a suspect, though they interviewed Faith MacLean *after* the inquest and recorded her description of this man. (The speculation about its being a woman came later.)

If the testimony of reliable witnesses proves that Mr. X was the murderer, the final question is: Can we deduce who he was?

In 1922, the second in command to District Attorney Thomas Lee Woolwine was his chief deputy, William C. Doran. After becoming a superior court judge in California in 1930, Doran reminisced about the case, stating that he had finally concluded there were only three motives for Taylor's murder: "The three principal motives for the Taylor murder were (1) a crime committed by a dope ring; (2) love and jealousy; and (3) revenge." Judge Doran's familiarity with the case and his position on the bench (he later served on the district court of appeal from 1935 to 1958) give added weight to his conclusions. He listed drugs first, though in 1922 neither he nor Woolwine nor any local official ever stated that this might be so. The explanation is that by 1930 the crisis that had produced the cover-up no longer existed. No federal attempt to regulate the movies had found support in Congress during the reign of Will Hays, and the crisis was a thing of the past.

Of the motives Judge Doran listed, there is more evidence for 1 than for the other two. The evidence includes Taylor's approach to the U.S. attorney for legal help in his fight against pushers; Taylor's fight with a drug dealer at the studio and with another at Mabel's house; his encounter with the menacing stranger on location, as reported by Theodore Kosloff; the statement by Captain E. A. Salisbury, and the evidence given by Mabel's friends and associates of her addiction. Taylor's interference with the drug ring's business made him a man marked for death. It is a reasonable conclusion that Mr. X was, in today's parlance, a contract killer, hit man, or executioner for the drug ring.

These words were, of course, unknown or at least unused in 1922, but "assassin" and "gangster" were widely used in this bootlegging era. According to the district attorney's office, between 1920 and 1933 there were at least twenty-eight assassinations in Los Angeles, many of them the toll of gangland territorial disputes.

It has been objected that Mr. X's actions were not those

of a professional hit man. He risked discovery by asking where Alvarado Court was located; apparently he took a trolley-car instead of using an automobile; he discarded cigarette stubs at the scene, and so on. This is all true, but he succeeded in his mission, the primary mark of a professional. He was evidently dispatched from out of town, and apparently arrived and left by train rather than plane. That is not the way it happens today on television, but this was 1922. Unfamiliar with Los Angeles geography, he would have been shown photos of Taylor—and apparently provided with cigarettes from his easily accessible stock—but had to ask exactly where Alvarado Court was. Though he may have risked discovery, the fact is that no one realized what he was up to until it was all over, a fact he may have been counting on.

He showed true professional brilliance at the single moment of real crisis. Having accomplished Taylor's murder without detection, having left the house with the smoking gun in his pocket, he emerged to find Faith MacLean in her doorway, looking straight at him. Instead of panicking, he solved the crisis by instantly going back to Taylor's door, pretending he'd forgotten something. His manner convinced Faith she had heard an auto backfiring. "I thought it was nothing, none of my business," she testified.

What if Judge Doran's alternative motives—love and jealousy or revenge—had been operative? A jealous lover would have known everything about Taylor, and would have needed no directions, even if he or she had hired a killer. Jealousy could not have been the motive. As for revenge, one writer speculated that an ex-soldier under Taylor's command, having resented his treatment in 1918, may have vowed to "get" Taylor, doing so four years later. There is no convincing evidence for this hypothesis, but assuming Mr. X was such a man, intent on personal revenge, the odds are that having performed an extremely emotional act after so long a lapse of time, he would have panicked at the sight of Faith MacLean.

The cool, unruffled behavior of the murderer is characteristic of the uninvolved professional. The accuracy of the word "uninvolved" is illustrated by a recent (1986) New York court case, in which an executioner named Luigi Ronsisvalle, hired by a heroin-smuggling gang, admitted he had murdered thirteen people, starting when he was eighteen years old. The attorney was determined to get this on record: "You've done it many times, too?" "Yes." "Thirteen separate times, sir. Right?" "Yessir.... It was not personal, sir." This expert assassin even explained in the witness box why he felt no guilt: "If you give me $30,000 to kill a person, *you* kill him, not me." *

Almost seventy years after William Desmond Taylor's murder, it is not likely that the name or identity of Mr. X will surface, nor is it probable that he is still alive. But at least we have solved the mystery to the extent of determining what he was—a hired executioner or contract killer.

* Shana Alexander, *The Pizza Connection: Lawyers, Money, Drugs, Mafia* (New York: Weidenfeld and Nicolson, 1988), pp. 123–4.

12

A Well-Directed Funeral

THE FUNERAL SERVICE of William Desmond Taylor took place at St. Paul's Pro-Cathedral in Hollywood on Tuesday, February 7, 1922. An enormous crowd, estimated at ten thousand, gathered in the streets. "Never before in the history of Los Angeles," wrote one reporter, "has there been such a crowd at the funeral of a private person." The police had difficulty in controlling the mob, which surged along Olive Street, overflowing into Pershing Square. Even after the beginning of the service, conducted by the Very Reverend William McCormack, Dean of St. Paul's, the mourners inside the church could hear the frightened cries of those who were caught outside in the crush, as a wave of pushing and shoving onlookers flowed right up to the church doors. The great crowd was attracted by the intensive publicity surrounding Taylor's murder, by morbid curiosity, and by the chance to see movie stars.

Since Taylor's young daughter, Ethel Daisy, was still

in New York and no family member was present to take charge, the funeral arrangements were entrusted to the Motion Picture Directors Association. Taylor's friend Frank Lloyd, a native of Scotland, staged the proceedings. (Lloyd, who directed Jackie Coogan in *Oliver Twist* in 1921, was later famous for films like *Cavalcade, Mutiny on the Bounty*, and *Blood on the Sun.*) He placed an empty director's chair, with Taylor's name on the back, in front of the catafalque. The coffin, on which Taylor's army captain's hat was placed, was covered with a Union Jack and rested on a costly carpet of American Beauty roses, the gift of Mabel Normand. A bouquet of Black Prince roses was placed near the coffin at the request of Mary Miles Minter, who did not attend the funeral. Floral pieces were sent by Gloria Swanson, Wallace Reid, Marshall Neilan, Rudolph Valentino, Betty Compson, and many others, all of whom were present at the service. Almost lost in the lavish display was a small bouquet of violets and lilies of the valley, bearing a card inscribed "With Ethel Daisy's love." A wreath of pink roses bore a card with the words "To my friend and fellow workman, God bless you," from Julia Crawford Ivers.

The arrival of Mabel Normand was dramatic. As her limousine pulled up to the entrance, the detectives guarding her wedged open a path through the crowd and accompanied her up the aisle to the section reserved for the film colony. She wore a fur coat, a hood, and a veil, and was sobbing. She was accompanied by a woman, probably Julia Brew, her nurse. George Hopkins, who sat in the pew with her, told King Vidor that Mabel never stopped crying, as if the finality of her lover's death had at last sunk in.

Among others present were Thomas Ince, who gave

The crowds at William Desmond Taylor's funeral.

Taylor his start in 1913; Cecil B. DeMille, Dustin Farnum and his wife, Winifred Kingston, Antonio Moreno, Edna Purviance, William Russell, Neva Gerber, Sessue Hayakawa, Julia Crawford Ivers, and Theodore Kosloff. Two members of Taylor's household staff, Henry Peavey and Howard Fellows, attended, as well as the latter's brother, Harold Fellows. The British Overseas Club attended as a group, and there was a contingent from the Motion Picture Directors Association.

The eight honorary pallbearers, marching behind the coffin to the strains of Handel's "Largo," were Charles Eyton, Frank Lloyd, Arthur Hoyt, William C. de Mille, James Young, David Hartford, Frank Beal, and George Melford. At the four corners of the catafalque an honor guard was posted, wearing uniforms of the Empire's armed forces—an English Tommy, soldiers from Canada and Australia, and a kilted Highlander. Considering that Taylor had reached the war zone after the Armistice, this was an unusual military tribute.

When the service was concluded, the guard of honor moved away and the casket was wheeled slowly up the aisle to the cathedral's vestibule, where Dean McCormack and the officiating ministers gathered. The mourners then filed slowly past the coffin to pay their last respects. Mabel Normand, who was almost last in the line, glanced briefly at the coffin, broke down completely, and swooned. She was helped to a rear pew, where she sat down with her companion.

The funeral procession of over one hundred automobiles drove slowly to the cemetery. A company of bagpipers in full regalia marched behind the hearse, and ordinary traffic was completely halted. The long line of cars followed Taylor's hearse to Santa Monica Boulevard, turning west to Hollywood Memorial Park Cemetery. As the coffin was placed in the crypt, the bagpipers played the eerie lament "Flowers of the Forest," a squad of soldiers fired a salute, and a bugler in naval uniform from the British warship *Calcutta*, anchored in the port of Los Angeles, sounded "The Last Post." It was a ceremony of which Major Kearns Deane-Tanner of the Carlow Rifles might have been proud.

Mabel Normand, who knew why Taylor was killed (but not who killed him), did not accompany the funeral cortege to the cemetery, though apparently she had intended to. While the organ pealed out the recessional and the mourners filed to their cars, she remained in one of the back pews, in a state of collapse. By the time the crowd had dispersed, she had recovered sufficiently to be taken home. The doctor ordered her to bed and forbade visitors. Her faithful pair of attendants, Mamie Owens and Julia Brew, watched over her. Julia, in whose arms she later died, said that near the end Mabel asked: "Julia, do you think they'll ever find out who killed Bill Taylor?"

At Ethel Daisy's order, the bronze plaque on the crypt in the mausoleum reads: "In Memory of William C. Deane-Tanner, Beloved Father of Ethel D. Deane-Tanner. Died February 1, 1922." This mausoleum also contains the crypts of Rudolph Valentino and Barbara La Marr. Nearby are the graves of Douglas Fairbanks, with its long reflecting pool, and of Virginia Rappe, whose death brought on the Arbuckle trials.

In the decades that followed, the Taylor case continued to reverberate. But, as Hollywood had hoped, the truth was buried with William Desmond Taylor.

Appendix: The Coroner's Inquest

The following is the transcript of the shorthand notes taken at the Coroner's inquest held on the body of William Desmond Taylor at Ivy H. Overholtzer [Mortuary] at Los Angeles, California on the 4th day of February, 1922 at 10:00 a.m.

FRANK A. NANCE, *Coroner*

Charles Eyton, being first duly sworn, testified as follows:

BY THE CORONER:

Q. Please state your name.

A. Charles Eyton.

Q. Where do you reside?

A. 1920 Vine Street, Hollywood.

Q. What is your occupation?

A. General Manager, Famous Players-Lasky Corporation.

Q. Mr. Eyton, have you seen the remains of the deceased in the adjoining room?

A. Yes, sir.

Q. Do you recognize them as one you knew in life?

241

A. Yes, sir.

Q. Who was it?

A. William Desmond Taylor.

Q. Where was he born?

A. He was born in Ireland, to the best of my knowledge. He told me so.

Q. What was his age?

A. Forty-four, I should judge. [*He was forty-nine.*]

Q. Was he married, single or a widower?

A. He was married. [*He was divorced as of 1916.*]

Q. When did he die?

A. Thursday morning or Wednesday night. I saw the body first on Thursday morning.

Q. Last Thursday?

A. Yes, sir.

Q. Do you recall that date?

A. It was the 2nd.

Q. February 2nd?

A. February 2nd.

Q. Where did he die?

A. At the Apartment "B," South Alvarado Street, 404 I think it was.

Q. What was the cause of his death, if you know?

A. Well, Mr. Taylor's assistant [*Harry Fellows*] rang me up at my residence about, I should judge, eight o'clock, and told me Mr. Taylor had died suddenly; so I immediately went over to his residence, and he was lying on the floor on his back. Detective Ziegler was there and he had called the doctor, he told me, previous to my arrival; and the doctor told me Mr. Taylor had died from hemorrhage of the stomach. Mr. MacLean—Douglas MacLean—had told me that he had thought he had heard a shot the night before, and his wife also thought she had heard a shot—and he wanted the body turned over; they didn't want to turn it over until the coroner came. The deputy coroner came after a while, and he told us he had died of hemorrhage of the stomach, and I told him he had better turn the body over to make sure, and he put his hand under Mr. Taylor's body, and found a little—when he pulled his hand out, it had a little blood on his hand. Douglas asked him what that was, and he said it evidently had run down from his [*Taylor's*] mouth, but I noticed that there was no trail of blood—Mr. Taylor's head was in a pool of blood— there was no trail of blood running down.

Q. There was a pool of blood under his head?

A. Under his head, yes, a little pool of blood. I immediately opened up Mr. Taylor's vest, and looked, and looked on the right-hand side, and there was no mark. I looked on the left-hand side and saw some blood, and then I told the Deputy Coroner that I thought that evidence enough to turn his body over to see what would happen. I sent for a pillow to put under Mr. Taylor's head, and we turned him over—the Deputy Coroner and myself—and we pulled his shirt and his vest up, and we found the bullet wound.

Q. Mr. Eyton, was his body stone cold at that time?

A. Stone cold and very stiff and rigid.

Q. Indicating that it had been dead for some time?

A. Yes.

Q. Where was the body lying with reference to the front entrance to his home?

A. It was lying right in front of a little desk with the head pointed east and the feet pointed west. I should judge the feet were three or four feet from the door—the front entrance.

Q. Who were present when you was there?

A. When I came in, the first man I noticed was Detective Ziegler, whom I have known for a number of years, and Douglas MacLean; Charles Maigne; the landlord [*E. C. Jessurun*]; and Harry Fellows, Mr. Taylor's assistant director.

Q. Did all of these persons live there in this neighborhood?

A. That I could not tell you. Mr. MacLean did, I know, be-cause he showed me where his apartment was.

Q. The place Mr. Taylor lived was in a court?

A. In a court, yes.

Q. These other buildings were nearby?

A. There are several apartments in this court, all the way around.

Q. Did Mr. and Mrs. MacLean, or either of them, tell you about the hour that they heard the gunshot?

A. Yes, Mr. MacLean told me it was about eight or a quar-ter after eight, and Mrs. MacLean thought it was a little later. [*This is not correct.*]

Q. That night?

A. Yes, the night before.

Q. You didn't make any definite measurements as to the position of the body?

A. No, sir.

Q. So that what you testified to is only an estimate, and nothing definite about it.

A. Yes.

Q. Now, how long has Mr. Taylor lived in this place?

A. That I could not tell you. He lived in it before he went to the war, I believe.

Q. When did you last see him alive?

A. The same day—Wednesday.

Q. Now, did he have any fire-arms of his own?

A. I believe he had a revolver; I believe the revolver was in the upper drawer upstairs; in fact, I know there was, because Detective Ziegler and myself went up there and saw it.

Q. When you were called to this place, did you see any fire-arms in this room where he was?

A. No.

Q. What is the name of his valet, or attendant there?

A. Harry Peavey, the colored cook. I never knew him or saw him.

Q. Was he the one who called you?

A. Harry Fellows, his assistant director, was the one who called me.

Q. You have no independent knowledge of the manner in which he met his death?

A. No, sir.

T H E   C O R O N E R : Have you any questions, gentlemen?

Q. (By a Juror)   Was his clothing ruffled in any way, showing any violence?

A. No, absolutely none; it looked like he just walked in the door and was shot in the back; that is the way it looked. It didn't show evidence in the room when I got there— neither the room or the body showed any evidence of a struggle. He had on the same suit as when I seen him the day before when he talked to me.

T H E   C O R O N E R : Is there any other questions? That is all, you may be excused.

Dr. A. F. Wagner, being first duly sworn, testified as follows:

Q. Please state your name.

A. Dr. A. F. Wagner.

Q. Where do you reside?

A. Los Angeles.

Q. What is your occupation?

A. Physician and County Autopsy Surgeon.

Q. Dr. Wagner, did you perform a post-mortem on the body of the deceased?

A. I did.

Q. Will you state your findings?

A. I performed an autopsy on William Desmond Taylor

at the morgue of Ivy H. Overholtzer, February 2, 1922 and found a bullet wound in the left side. The bullet entered six and a half inches below the armpit, and in the posterior axillary line, and passed inward and upward, passing through the seventh interspace of the ribs, penetrating both lobes of the left lung, and emerging on the inner margin of the left lobe, then traversing the mediastinum, passed out of the chest on the right side of the middle line, posterior to the right collar bone, and entered the tissues of the neck; and I found the bullet just beneath the skin, four and a half inches to the left of the outer side of the right shoulder, and on a line drawn from the top of the shoulder to the lower junction of the right ear. The left pleural cavity contained considerable clotted blood. The vital, chest, and abdominal organs were free from disease. The cause of death was gunshot wound of the chest.

THE CORONER: Have you any questions, gentlemen? That is all, you may be excused.

Mabel Normand, being first duly sworn, testified as follows:

Q.   Please state your name.
A.   Mabel Normand.
Q.   Where do you reside?
A.   3089 West Seventh.
Q.   What is your occupation?
A.   Motion pictures.
Q.   Miss Normand, were you acquainted with Mr. Taylor, the deceased in this case?
A.   Yes.
Q.   Did you see him on the evening before his death occurred?
A.   Yes, I did.

Q. And where did you see him?

A. Will I tell you when I went in there and when I came out?

Q. Did you see him at his home?

A. Oh, yes.

Q. And you were with him about how long on that occasion?

A. I got there about 7 o'clock, and left at a quarter to 8.

Q. And when you left his place, did you leave him in the house, or outside?

A. No, he came to my car with me.

Q. Where was your car?

A. Right in front of the court.

Q. On Alvarado Street?

A. Yes, on the hill.

Q. He accompanied you to your car?

A. Yes.

Q. Was he still there when you drove away?

A. Yes, as my car turned around, I waived my hand at him; he was partly up the little stairs there.

Q. At the time you was in the house, was anybody else in the house?

A. Yes, Henry, his man.

Q. Henry Peavey?

A. Yes.

Q. Do you know whether Mr. Peavey left the house before you did or not?

A. Yes, he did; he left about, I should say, about 15 or 20 minutes before I left, but stopped outside and spoke to my chauffeur; we came out later.

Q. No one else except Henry Peavey was there?

A. That was all.

Q. What time was it you say you left him—drove away from his place?

A. I left him on the sidewalk about a quarter to eight.

Q. Did you expect to see him or hear from him later that evening?

A. Yes, he said—he had finished his dinner—he said would I go out and take dinner with him and I said no, I was tired; I had to go home and get up very early; he said he would call me up in about an hour.

Q. Did he call you?

A. No, I went to bed; if he called me I was asleep; when I am asleep he tells my maid not to disturb me.

Q. Was that the last time you saw him, when you left him about a quarter to eight?

A. That was the last time.

THE CORONER: Have you any questions, gentlemen? That is all, you may be excused.

Henry Peavey, being first duly sworn, testified as follows:

Q. Please state your name.

A. Henry Peavey.

Q. Where do you live?

A. I live at 127½ East 3rd Street.

Q. What is your occupation?

A. Cook and valet.

Q. Mr. Peavey, were you employed by Mr. Taylor, the deceased in this case?

A. Sir?

Q. Were you employed by the dead man in the case?

A. Yes, sir.

Q. How long have you been working for him?

A. About six months.

Q. Were you in the house on the evening when he was found dead there?

A. Yes, sir.

Q. What time did you leave the house?

A. I figured it was about a quarter past [seven] that I left the house.

Q. Where was he when you left?

A. He was sitting in a chair facing just to the [illegible] now, and Miss Normand was sitting in a chair just the same. They were discussing a red-backed book.

Q. In what part of the house were they?

A. They were near the dining-room, where you enter the dining-room from the living-room.

Q. That is a two-story apartment, is it not?

A. Yes, sir.

Q. And on the ground floor, how many rooms?

A. The living-room, dining-room and kitchen.

Q. Now, the entrance to this apartment is immediately into the front there, is it not—the front room, rather?

A. The front room, yes sir.

Q. They were seated?

A. Near the dining-room there, in the living-room, near the entrance to the dining-room.

Q. When you went out, which way did you go out, at the front or the back?

A. I went out the front way. I always lock up the back door when I go out. I always lock the back door screen; it has a hook on the inside. I used the front door to come out all the time.

Q. Did you carry the back door key with you?

A. No, sir. I always turn it in the door and leave it just as it is.

Q. Now, when did you next see Mr. Taylor?

A. The next morning, when I went to work.

Q. What time are you in the habit of coming to work?

A. I am usually there about half past seven.

Q. What time did you arrive there the next morning?

A. At just about half past seven.

Q. What day was that?

A. Thursday morning [*February 2*].

Q. On arriving there, what did you do?

A. I picked up the paper first; I stopped in a drug store at the corner of 5th and Los Angeles to get a bottle of medicine—milk of magnesia, he usually takes that every morning; I bought that on my way out. I picked up the paper and unlocked the door. The first thing I saw was his feet. I looked at his feet a few minutes and said, "Mr. Taylor." He never moved. I stepped a little further in the door, and seen his face, and turned and ran out and hollered.

Q. Who did you summon? Who did you call to?
A. I don't know.
Q. You just made a lot of noise to attract all the attention you could?
A. Yes, sir.
Q. Several people came, did they?
A. Yes, sir. I think Mr. Desmond [*sic*], and the gentleman who owns the court was the first.
Q. You mean Mr. Jessurun?
A. Yes, sir.
Q. Who else came?
A. And Mr.—you see, I don't know their names—I just seen them—the two gentlemens next door, Mr. Mac-Lean and Mr.—I can't think of the other gentleman's name—right next door to us [*Charles Maigne*].
Q. You didn't come back there after you had gone away, when Miss Normand was there with Mr. Taylor?
A. No, sir.
Q. When you went out, was anybody around the place?
A. Only Miss Normand's chauffeur; he had his lights all on inside the limousine, cleaning it. I hit him on the back and stopped and talked to him a few minutes.
Q. When you first opened the door, did you see any furniture overturned, or any sign of a disturbance in the house?
A. Nothing more than a chair that was sitting next to the wall had been pushed out a little bit and his feet was under this chair. The rest of the furniture around the house and room upstairs was just as I

left them when I went away that evening.

Q. And did you notice whether anything had been taken off of his body, or not—any jewelry?

A. I didn't notice that; I didn't touch him at all.

Q. Do you know whether he wore any valuable jewelry?

A. Yes sir, he had a wrist watch and another watch with a lot of little trinkets on; and a thing you stamp checks with to keep anybody from making the checks any bigger, and a lead pencil.

Q. Did he have a diamond ring?

A. Yes sir, he had a large diamond ring that he wore.

Q. Do you know whether he had it on that evening?

A. Yes sir, he was dressed just as when I went that evening, as I found him the next morning.

Q. Was the ring on his finger the next morning?

A. Yes sir, his other jewelry that I had put away the night before was just as I had put it away up in the dresser drawer.

Q. You didn't find anything taken from the apartment?

A. No sir, it was just as when I left it when I found it. The rug was a little bit kicked up. It looked like he had kicked it with his foot.

Q. There was no other disturbance there?

A. No, sir. Even the living-room table that I had moved aside. The rocking chair would hit the table, and I moved the table so the rocking chair would not hit the table. It was just as I left it.

Q. By a juror: Were any of the windows up at night?

A. No sir, we had those little long pins that runs in the windows. The windows upstairs in his bedroom were up. The windows downstairs I always locked with this peg that slipped in the window.

Q. Were they still that way in the morning?

A. They were still that way in the morning. The lights were burning just as I had left them that night; two lights, one in the living-room and one in the dining-room.

Appendix: The Coroner's Inquest

CORONER: That is all, you may be excused.

T. H. Ziegler, being first duly sworn, testified as follows:

BY THE CORONER:

Q. Please state your name.
A. T. H. Ziegler.
Q. Where do you live?
A. 425 North Hill.
Q. What is your occupation?
A. Police officer.
Q. Mr. Ziegler, were you called to the premises when the deceased was found dead?
A. I was.
Q. When did you arrive there?
A. A little before 8 o'clock in the morning of February 2nd.
Q. Will you state what you found when you got there?
A. I found the deceased, Mr. Taylor, lying just inside of the door, on his back. His hands, one of them, apparently to the side of his body, and the other lying outstretched; and blood pouring from his mouth. He was lying with his head to the east, flat on his back, dead.
Q. Was his body rigid and cold?
A. It was.
Q. Indicating he had been dead for some time?
A. Yes, sir.
Q. Did you see any evidence of a disturbance in the house?
A. Not any.
Q. Who was there when you arrived there?
A. The owner of the building; Mr. MacLean; another movie actor [*Charles Maigne*], and Peavey.
Q. You mean the owner of the building, Mr. Jessurun?
A. Yes, sir, and Mr. MacLean and another man I don't know.
Q. One of the adjacent tenants of the building?

A. Yes sir, living next door east of Mr. Taylor.

Q. Did you question any of those persons as to whether they had heard any gunshot the night previous?

A. I did. I learned that from Mrs. MacLean, that along about fifteen or perhaps ten minutes to eight, the night before, she heard a shot. She thought it was a gunshot. She went to her front door and opened the door, and saw a man standing in Mr. Taylor's door. She looked at him, and he stood and looked at her; and he walked down the steps, turned to the left, and going around the end of the building, which is to the east; and out into the street.

Q. Into what street?

A. Which is Maryland, I think.

Q. Did Mr. Jessurun tell you he heard a shot?

A. I think he did.

Q. Did he say why he didn't try to investigate it?

A. He did not. He didn't know but what it was an automobile making a noise.

Q. Did Mr. MacLean endeavor to investigate it?

A. Not that I know of, and Mrs. MacLean's maid also heard a shot.

Q. Did they say why they didn't attempt to investigate the cause of the shot?

A. They did not.

Q. Did you find any weapon about the room where the deceased was lying?

A. I found a weapon in the room above.

Q. Where was it?

A. In the front bedroom in the dresser drawer, lying on a sort of box.

Q. Did you investigate to see whether the clothing was powder burnt or not?

A. I did not. That was investigated, I understand, later.

Q. Did you ask any of the persons who were called by

Henry Peavey, the valet, whether there was any weapon there when they first came into the room?

A. Yes, sir. We looked for everything of that kind.

Q. Have you formed any conclusion whether it was possible this shot could have been fired by the deceased himself?

A. Impossible.

T H E C O R O N E R : Have you any questions, gentlemen?

Q. By a juror: Was the revolver found upstairs loaded?

A. It was. It had five shells in it; it had not been shot of late.

Q. Was it the same caliber bullet as was found on the deceased?

A. This was a .32 automatic Savage.

Q. In the drawer upstairs?

A. Yes.

Q. What was the number of the bullet that was found?

A. I understand that it was a .38. I haven't seen it.

T H E C O R O N E R : That is all, you may be excused. That is all the evidence we will take in this case. All but the Jury will be excused.

I hereby certify that I, as shorthand reporter, correctly took down in shorthand the testimony and proceedings had at the within named Coroner's inquest; that the foregoing is a full, true and correct copy of my shorthand notes and a full, true and correct statement of the testimony and proceedings had at said inquest.

E. M. ALLEN, *Shorthand Reporter*

Acknowledgments

I thank Shakespeare for my title, which comes from Titus's words to Marcus in *Titus Andronicus*, II, ii, 56: "A deed of death, done on the innocent." It seems especially apt because William Desmond Taylor, the victim, was himself innocent of crime. The Hollywood crisis of 1922 was so serious that the producers decided, in King Vidor's words, that "They'd rather sacrifice Taylor than sacrifice the whole industry." The only thanks Taylor got for his fight against drugs in Hollywood was a besmeared reputation. I hope this book will help to restore his good name.

To Bruce Long of Tempe, Arizona, the editor and publisher of a newsletter, *Taylorology*, filled with facts and details of the case culled from contemporary records, I owe a special debt. Naturally he and I did not always agree on the interpretation of every item, but his concern for accuracy and his generous assistance have been invaluable.

To Betty Harper Fussell, whose biography of Mabel Normand is the fullest and best-written account of this tragic star of the silents, I am grateful for many favors. I believe she was the first person to obtain from the elusive Los Angeles authorities a transcript of Taylor's inquest, which she shared with me.

To Liam O'Leary of Dublin, author of *Rex Ingram: Master of the Silent Cinema*, I am indebted for tracking down the birth records of the Deane-Tanner family in Cork, the first really accurate information about William Desmond Taylor's origins.

To Kemp Niver and his associate Bebe Bergsten, for restoring and cataloguing the early Biograph and D. W. Griffith prints at the Library of Congress; * for their carefully edited series of early film history books; for providing me with the unlisted number of Mary Miles Minter, and for other friendly favors.

To Eileen Bowser of the Museum of Modern Art Film Library, I am grateful for screenings of Mabel Normand's *Mickey* and Blanche Sweet and William Russell's *Anna Christie*; and to Jan-Christopher Horak of the George Eastman House in Rochester, for screening William Desmond Taylor's *Huckleberry Finn*.

To Marc Wanamaker of Bison Archives I owe thanks for his generous help in locating early photographs and in providing prints and negatives for this book. To Stephen Normand, from whom I learned a great deal about his grand-aunt's career and the Normand family background, I am indebted for the courtesy of stills and other documents. To John Kobal, author of *People Will Talk* (the best collection of movie interviews I know of), thanks for the loan of two rare stills from his book *Hollywood: The Years of Innocence*.

To Tom McDonald, chief field deputy, Bureau of Public Affairs, Office of the Los Angeles District Attorney, I am grateful for information about Thomas Lee Woolwine; and to Margaret A. Smith, attorney in charge, Freedom of In-

* These early movies survived only because the pioneer movie-makers, interpreting copyright law literally, had deposited complete positive printed rolls of movies, frame by frame, in Washington. They were beginning to crumble when, decades later, Kemp Niver made it possible to restore most of them for projection.

formation Unit, Office of the Assistant Attorney General, U. S. Department of Justice, whose statement of March 10, 1989, that "This office has nothing to provide" I acknowledge.

To departed friends I owe thanks for encouraging my interest in movie history from the start: James Agee, DeWitt Bodeen, Otis Ferguson, James Shelley Hamilton, Theodore Huff, Jay Leyda, Dwight Macdonald, J. K. Paulding, Blanche Sweet, William Troy, Mark Van Doren, and King Vidor.

To a number of friends and associates, I owe my thanks for early readings of the manuscript and many suggestions for improving the text—namely Harry Ford, Linda Healey, Paul Horgan, Hugh James McKenna, Charles Phillips Reilly, Eileen Simpson, Thomas Stewart, William Verdon, Arthur W. Wang, and Lynn Warshow.

Bibliography

Anslinger, Harry J. *The Murderers: The Story of the Narcotic Gangs*. New York: Farrar, Straus & Giroux, 1961.

Barry, Iris. *Let's Go to the Movies*. London: Chatto & Windus, 1926.

Barry, Iris, and Eileen Bowser. *D. W. Griffith*. New York: Museum of Modern Art, 1965.

Berg, A. Scott. *Goldwyn: A Biography*. New York: Alfred A. Knopf, 1989.

Bitzer, Billy. *His Story*. Introduction by Beaumont Newhall. New York: Farrar, Straus & Giroux, 1973.

Bodeen, DeWitt (pseud. "Aydelott Ames"). "Mary Miles Minter," in *Films in Review*, October 1969.

Bogdanovich, Peter. *Allan Dwan: The Last Pioneer*. New York and London: Praeger, 1971.

Bowser, Eileen, ed. *Biograph Bulletins: 1908–1912*. New York: Octagon Books, 1973.

Bibliography

Brown, Karl. *Adventures with D. W. Griffith.* Edited and introduced by Kevin Brownlow. New York: Farrar, Straus & Giroux, 1973.

Brownlow, Kevin. *The Parade's Gone By.* New York: Alfred A. Knopf, 1968.

————. *The War, the West, and the Wilderness.* Alfred A. Knopf, 1978.

————. *Hollywood: The Pioneers.* New York: Alfred A. Knopf, 1979.

Bumpus, G. M. *The Man Who Killed William Desmond Taylor.* Gardena, Calif.: Logan Dillon, 1945.

Chaplin, Charles. *My Autobiography.* New York: Simon & Schuster, 1964.

Cooper, Miriam. *Dark Lady of the Silents.* Indianapolis: Bobbs-Merrill, 1973.

Doherty, Edward. *Gall and Honey.* New York: Sheed & Ward, 1941.

DuMain, Ken. "Correcting Misinformation About Miss Mary Miles Minter," in *Films in Review*, May 1985.

Everson, William K. *American Silent Film.* New York: Oxford University Press, 1978.

Faure, Elie. *The Art of Cineplastics.* Translated by Walter Pach. Boston: Four Seas Company, 1923.

Florey, Robert. *Quatre Stars.* Paris: Jean-Pascal, 1927.

Fowler, Gene. *Father Goose: The Story of Mack Sennett.* New York: Covici, Friede, 1934.

Friedrich, Otto. *City of Nets.* New York: Harper & Row, 1986.

Fussell, Betty Harper. *Mabel.* New York and New Haven: Ticknor & Fields, 1982.

Gardner, Erle Stanley. "William Desmond Taylor," in *The Los Angeles Murders*, Craig Rice, ed. New York: Duell, Sloan & Pearce, 1947.

Giroux, Robert. "Mack Sennett," in *Films in Review*, December 1968, January 1969.

———. "The Farce of *A Cast of Killers*," in *Films in Review*, November 1986.

Goldwyn, Samuel. *Behind the Screen*. New York: George H. Doran, 1923.

Griffith, Mrs. D. W. *When the Movies Were Young*. New York: Dutton, 1925.

Hampton, Benjamin B. *A History of the Movies*. New York: Covici, Friede, 1931.

Hawtry, Sir Charles. *The Truth at Last*. Edited and introduced by W. Somerset Maugham. Boston: Little, Brown, 1924.

Hays, Will H. *Memoirs of Will H. Hays*. New York: Doubleday, 1955.

Higham, Charles. *Celebrity Circus*. New York: Delacorte, 1979.

Hopper, Hedda. *From Under My Hat*. New York: Doubleday, 1952.

Jobes, Gertrude. *Motion Picture Empire*. Hamden, Conn.: Archon Books, 1966.

Jones, Grover. "Magic Lantern," in *Saturday Evening Post*, January 23, 1937.

King, Lieut. Edward C. "I Know Who Killed Desmond Taylor," in *True Detective Mysteries*, September, October 1930.

Kirkpatrick, Sidney D. *A Cast of Killers*. New York: Dutton, 1986.

Knoblock, Edward. *Round the Room.* London: Chapman & Hall, 1939.

Kobal, John. *Hollywood: The Years of Innocence.* New York: Abbeville Press, 1985.

―――. *People Will Talk.* New York: Alfred A. Knopf, 1985.

Lahue, Kalton C. *Dreams for Sale: The Rise and Fall of the Triangle Corporation.* New York: A. S. Barnes, 1971.

Lasky, Jesse L. *I Blow My Own Horn.* New York: Doubleday, 1957.

Lejeune, C. A. *Cinema.* London: Alexander Maclehose, 1931.

Leyda, Jay. *Kino: A History of the Russian and Soviet Film.* New York: Macmillan; London: Allen & Unwin, 1960.

Lindsay, Vachel. *The Art of the Moving Picture.* New York: Macmillan, 1915.

Long, Bruce. "The William Desmond Taylor Murder Case," in *Classic Film Collector*, no. 57 (Winter 1977).

―――. *Taylorology* (newsletter), no. 1 (Fall 1985), no. 2 (Spring 1986).

Loos, Anita. *A Girl Like I.* New York: Viking, 1966.

Lusk, Norbert. "I Love Actresses!" in *New Movies*, Richard Griffith, ed. New York: National Board of Review, March 1946–April 1948.

McCardell, Roy L. *The Diamond From the Sky.* New York: G. W. Dillingham, 1916.

Marion, Frances. *Off With Their Heads!* New York: Macmillan, 1972.

Marsh, Mae. *Screen Acting.* New York: Stokes, 1921.

Mesguich, Félix. *Tours de Manivelle: Souvenirs d'un Chasseur d'Images.* Préface de Louis Lumière. Paris: Grasset, 1933.

Morgan, Ted. *Maugham.* New York: Simon & Schuster, 1980.

Moussinac, Léon. *Naissance du Cinéma.* Paris: J. Povolozky, 1925.

Muir, Florabel. *Headline Happy.* New York: Henry Holt, 1950.

Munsterberg, Hugo. *The Photoplay: A Psychological Study.* New York: Appleton, 1916.

Niver, Kemp, and Bebe Bergsten, eds. *Biograph Bulletins: 1896–1908.* Los Angeles: Locare Research Group, 1971.

Normand, Stephen. "Mabel Normand," in *Films in Review,* August–September 1974.

Odell, George. *Annals of the New York Stage.* Vol. 15. New York: Columbia University Press, 1936.

Pratt, George C. *Spellbound in Darkness: A History of the Silent Film.* Greenwich, Conn.: New York Graphic Society, 1973.

Ramsaye, Terry. *A Million and One Nights: A History of the Motion Picture.* 2 vols. New York: Simon & Schuster, 1926.

Reid, Mrs. Bertha Westbrook. *Wallace Reid: His Life Story by His Mother.* New York: Sorg Publishing Co., 1923.

Rosenberg, Bernard, and Harry Silverstein, eds. *The Real Tinsel.* New York: Macmillan, 1970.

Rotha, Paul. *The Film Till Now.* London: Jonathan Cape, 1930.

St. Johns, Adela Rogers. *The Honeycomb.* New York: Doubleday, 1969.

Seale, Jim. "A Cast of Liars," in *Los Angeles Magazine*, January 1987.

Sennett, Mack. *King of Comedy*. New York: Doubleday, 1954.

Sherwood, Robert. *The Best Moving Pictures of 1922–1923*. Boston: Small, Maynard, 1923.

Sillman, Leonard. *Here Lies Leonard Sillman*. New York: Citadel, 1959.

Simenon, Georges. *La Tête d'un Homme*. Translated by Geoffrey Sainsbury as *Maigret's War of Nerves*. New York: Harcourt Brace Jovanovich, 1986.

Slide, Anthony. *Early Women Directors*. New York: A. S. Barnes, 1977.

Slide, Anthony, and Edward Wagenknecht. *Fifty Great American Silent Films, 1912–1920*. New York: Dover, 1980.

Spehr, Paul C. *The Movies Begin: Making Movies in New Jersey, 1887–1920*. Newark, N.J.: The Newark Museum, 1977.

Starks, Michael. *Cocaine Fiends and Reefer Madness: An Illustrated History of Drugs in the Movies*. New York: Cornwall Books, 1982.

Sutherland, Sidney. "Mabel Normand, Comedienne and Madcap," in *Liberty*, September 27, October 4, 11, 18, 25, November 1, 1930.

Swanson, Gloria. *Swanson on Swanson*. New York: Random House, 1980.

Torrence, Bruce T. *Hollywood: The First Hundred Years*. New York: Zoetrope, 1982.

Vidor, King. *A Tree Is a Tree*. New York: Harcourt, Brace, 1953.

Wagenknecht, Edward. *The Movies in the Age of Innocence.* Norman: University of Oklahoma Press, 1962.

Wagner, Rob. *Film Folk.* New York: Century, 1918.

Weaver, John T., ed. *Twenty Years of the Silents: 1908–1928.* Metuchen, N.J.: The Scarecrow Press, 1971.

Welsh, Robert E. *A-B-C of Motion Pictures.* New York: Harper, 1916.

Whitton, Douglas J. "Mystery Woman Director" [Julia Crawford Ivers], in *Classic Images,* no. 121 (July 1985).

Wid, ed. (F. C. Gunning). *Wid's Year Book 1920–1921, Wid's Year Book 1921–1922, Film Year Book 1922–1923.* New York: Arno Press, 1971.

Yallop, David. *The Day the Laughter Stopped: The True Story of Fatty Arbuckle.* New York: St. Martin's Press, 1976.

Index

Page numbers in *italics* indicate illustrations.

Index

England, 52, 54–5, 87, 105, 118, 120, 176
Enoch Arden, 41
Espionage Act, 104
Essanay, 189
Everson, William K., 107, 110; *American Silent Film*, 35 and *n*.
Eyes of Julia Deep, The, 144
Eyton, Charles, 9, 10–11, 17, 46, 98, 163–5, 175, 227, 238, 241–5

Fairbanks, Douglas, xviii, 32, 118, 239
Famous Players–Lasky Paramount, 6, 107, 163, 192, 241
Farnum, Dustin, 47, 93, 103, 141, 238
Farnum, William, 141
Farrar, Geraldine, 41
Faye, Hughie, 198
Federal Bureau of Narcotics, 32, 199, 211, 214
Fédora, 59
Fellows, Harry, 9, *115*, 238, 242, 243, 245
Fellows, Howard, 8–9, 17, 117, 206, 228, 238
Ferguson, Elsie, 41, 103, *119*
Fillmore, Hugh Hamilton, 155
Fillmore, Margaret Shelby, 136, 147, 154–6, 159
Finch, Flora, 182
Fitts, District Attorney Buron, 130, 157, 159
Flagg, James Montgomery, 182
Fleming, Victor, 87
Floor Below, The, 197
Floradora, 62, 64
Flying "A," 87, 88, 91, 94, 142

Foolish Wives, 35
Fools First, 135
Forever, 41
Fox, William, 35
France, Anatole, 188
Francisco, Betty, 135
Freedom of Information Act, 214
Freud, Sigmund, 24, 188
Frohman, Charles, 141
funeral service, 235–6, *237*, 238-9
Furnace, The, 104, 135
Fussell, Betty Harper, 198; *Mabel*, 191 and *n*., 230 and *n*.

Garbo, Greta, 76
Garbutt, Frank C., 97, 98
Garden, Mary, 192
Gardner, Erle Stanley, xvi
Gerber, Neva, 9, 53, 66, 79–80, *81*, 82, 84, 86–7, 92, 95, 117, 132, 238
Ghost of Rosy Taylor, The, 144
Gish, Lillian, 41
Gismonda, 59
Goldstein, Robert, 104
Goldwyn, Samuel, xviii, 35, 94, 98, 190, 191, 192–3, *194*, 195, *196*, 197–202, 221; *Behind the Screen*, 195 and *n*.
Goldwyn Motion Picture Company, 192
Gone With the Wind, 87
Gonzales, Myrtle, 79
Goode, Will B. (Fatty Arbuckle), 40
Goodrich, William (Fatty Arbuckle), 40

Index

Lloyd, Harold, 24, 28
Loew, Marcus, 35
Long Beach Press, 127
Loos, Anita, 31, 199–200; *A Girl Like I*, 200n.
Los Angeles Examiner, 37, 101, 128, 135, 157
Los Angeles Record, 56, 138, 139
Los Angeles Times, 127, 137, 145
Louÿs, Pierre, 188
Love, Bessie, 44
love letter to Taylor from Mary Miles Minter, 46–7, *48*
Lowe, Edmund, 99, 103
Lumière, Louis and Auguste, xiv–xv

Mabel at the Wheel, 190
Mabel Normand Film Company, 189, 191
MacDonald, William, 10, 17, 165
MacLean, Douglas, 6, 8, 9–10, 11, 13–17, 103, 112, 163, 172, 226, 242, 243, 244, 250, 252, 253
MacLean, Faith, 8, 9, 11, 13–17, 100, 117, 127, 162, 163, 164, 172, 173, 214, 226, 227–8, 230, 231, 233, 234, 244, 253
MacPherson, Jeanie, 96
Maigne, Charles, 6, 8, 163, 243, 250, 252
Making a Living, 183
Marion, Frances, 96
Marsh, Edward, 134
Marsh, Mae, 192, 201
Mathews, Frances Aymar, 59

Maugham, Somerset, 55, *119*, 132, 134
May, Luke S., 128
Mayer, Louis B., 36, 142
McAvoy, May, 103, *133*
McCardell, Roy L., 88; *The Diamond From the Sky: A Romantic Novel*, 90 and *n.*
McCarthy, Neil, 154
Melford, George, 238
Mencken, H. L., 140
Menjou, Adolphe, 7
Merton of the Movies, 157
Mesguich, Félix, *Tours de Manivelle*, xv *n.*
Metro Pictures, 142, *143*
Mickey, 189, 191–2, 193
Mile-a-Minute Kendall, 103
Miller, Lillian, 34
Minter, Mary Miles, xvi–xviii, 6, 9, 18, *42*, 45–7, *49*, 94, 103, 104*n.*, 107, 114, 117, 136–42, *143*, 144–7, *148*, 149–51, *152*, 153–7, *158*, 159–61, 163, 230, 236
Mitchell, Rhea "Ginger," 72
M'Liss, 114
Moore, Colleen, 114
Morals, 104, *133*
Moreno, Antonio, 26, 112, 117, 135, 238
Morgan, Ted, *Maugham*, 134n.
Morosco, Oliver, 97, 112
Morosco-Bosworth Studios, 97–8
Morosco Pictures, 97–8
Motion Picture Directors Association, 6, 87, 107, 236, 238
Motion Picture News, 142

271

Index

Index

A Note About the Author

ROBERT GIROUX is a bookman—editor, publisher, writer, and reader. He has been associated with Farrar, Straus & Giroux since 1955 and has worked with some of the most eminent writers of our time. In 1987 he won the National Book Critics Circle award "for his distinguished contributions to American literature as editor and publisher."

A Note on the Type

The text of this book was set on the Linotype in Bodoni Book,
a typeface named for Giambattista Bodoni, who was born
in Saluzzo, Piedmont, in 1740. He was the son of a printer,
and as a young man went to Rome, where he served as an
apprentice at the press of the Propaganda Fide. In 1768 he was
put in charge of the Stamperia Reale in Parma by Duke
Ferdinand, which position he held until his death in 1813, in
spite of many offers by royal patrons to tempt him elsewhere. His
earliest types were those imported from the Paris foundry of
Fournier, but gradually these were superseded by his own
designs, which, in the many distinguished books he printed,
became famous all over Europe. His later arrangements with the
Duke allowed him to print for anyone who would employ him,
and commissions flowed in, so that he was able to produce
books in French, Russian, German, and English, as well as
Italian, Greek, and Latin. His *Manuale Tipografico*, issued in
1818 by his widow, is one of the finest specimen books issued
by a printer-type designer.

Composed by Heritage Printers, Charlotte, North Carolina
Printed and bound by The Murray Printing Company,
Westford, Massachusetts
Designed by Harry Ford